BUMPER QUIZ BOOK FOR THE FAMILY

Ken Russell and Philip Carter

Michael O'Mara Books Limited

First published in Great Britain in 1998 by
Michael O'Mara Books Limited
9 Lion Yard, Tremadoc Road
London SW4 7NQ

A CIP catalogue record for this book is available
from the British Library

ISBN 1-85479-329-2

1 3 5 7 9 10 8 6 4 2

Designed and typeset by Martin Bristow

Printed and bound in Finland by WSOY

CONTENTS

PUZZLES

VEGETABLES

The four 9-letter words have been jumbled. Solve the four anagrams of vegetables and then transfer the letters indicated by the shaded squares to the Key Anagram, rearranging them to find a fifth vegetable. Two of the vegetables are a type of pea.

| I | H | A | T | E | R | O | C | K |

| S |
| P |
| U |
| R |
| A |
| S |
| A |
| G |
| A |

| R |
| A |
| W |
| F |
| O |
| R |
| M |
| A |
| T |

| R | U | E | A | B | I | N | G | E |

Key Anagram

PAUL'S AGE

Paul was 20 years old in 1990 but only 15 years old in 1995. How is this possible?

ORONYMS

An oronym is a sentence or phrase that can be read in two ways, has the same sound, but has different spellings.
For example: a name / an aim.
Find a pair of oronyms from each pair of given clues.
Example: An idea; Atlantic
Answer: A notion; an ocean

1. Pleasant person; a very cold person
2. Large primate; colourless ribbon
3. First-class result; dull time period
4. I yell; sweetened frozen liquid
5. Spring bark; abscond
6. Tariff during hours of darkness; acidic salt
7. Fruit-filled pastry; swollen organ of sight
8. Measuring and calculating instrument; crafty drivel
9. Spring flowers; facial feature
10. A number of singles; a number of feeble birds
11. Accursed dowels; slightly wet ovum
12. I smell; chilled writing material

ALL CHANGE

Work out the following phrases which have all been disguised by altering one letter in each word.
For example:
Find any candy = Fine and dandy

1. hare I dug it
2. go form but
3. end to forty
4. as I goose and
5. dear pet
6. read ever heeds
7. so pay town she lad
8. on too minks
9. puts any boots
10. bop on she Pope
11. pout on calf
12. rake is dead
13. read line
14. do ever us
15. so fail feat
16. all an case
17. no core so fight
18. row end when
19. an she back
20. do so no set

SOMETHING IN COMMON

What do these six words have in common?

EMOTIONLESS

GASTRONOMICALLY

VINDICATION

BLITHESOME

TREASONABLE

REVOLUTIONARY

MAGIC CUBE

Complete the cube with 15 five-letter words. Each face of the cube contains 5 five-letter words which read the same both across and down.
Clues to the 15 five-letter words you are seeking are given below, but in no particular order.

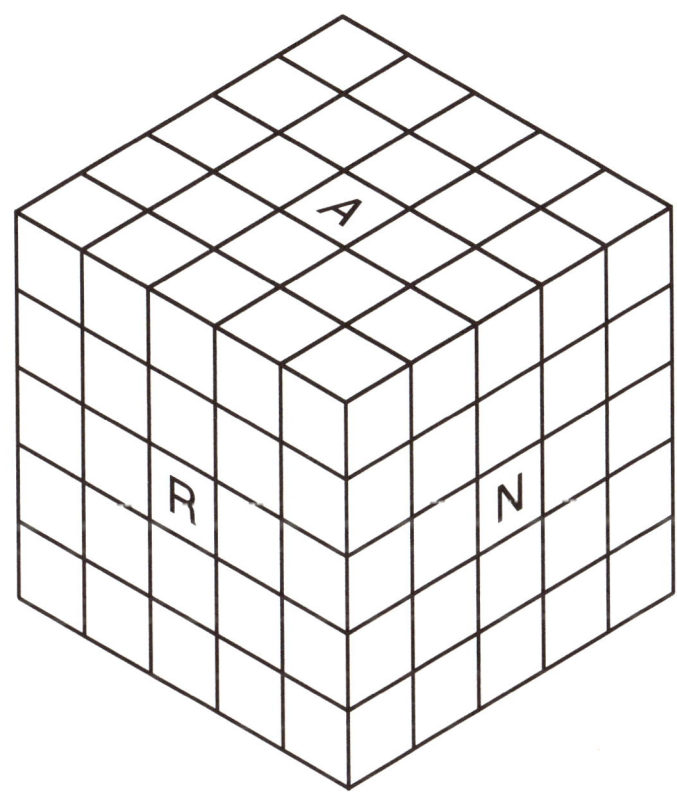

CLUES

Warehouse
Nurse Cavell
Additional
Out of order
Speak formally
Russian revolutionary leader
Without clothes
Greek teller of fables

African horned mammal
Perception
Collection of maps
Writing material
Idea or topic
Positive electrode
Strip of leather

VEHICLES

The four nine-letter words have been jumbled. Solve the four anagrams of types of vehicles and then transfer the letters indicated by the shaded squares to the Key Anagram, rearranging them to find a fifth vehicle.

R A V E N L O R D

S C R A P S R O T

B U L B B R A C E

I E M U L S I O N

Key Anagram

8

THREESOMES

Use each letter once only in the following five phrases to spell out three of a kind:

1. Three colours:

GAINED ON BORROWING

2. Three dances:

GLOW BUM AT TARZAN

3. Three sports:

ANGER FILTHY CENSOR

4. Three capital cities:

DATED A WOMANISH TART

5. Three animals:

FINE AEROPLANE FLIGHT

BACKWARDS AND FORWARDS

Words run forwards then backwards using the three letters of the previous word, as in the example shown:

1–2 BOILED; 2–3 DELVED

Two words appear twice in the answers list.

1–2	Bubbled
2–3	Investigated
3–4	Bereft
4–5	Semiconductor devices
5–6	Handsome cabs
6–7	Trapped
7–8	Insecticide
8–9	Bright heavenly star
9–10	Wooer
10–11	Corrupt
11–12	Lower region
12–13	Repair shoe
13–14	Ogled
14–15	Disdain
15–16	Inventor of the light bulb
16–17	Genus of gelatinous freshwater algae
17–18	White, downy fibre
18–19	Idea
19–20	Sounds
20–21	The last six lines of a sonnet
21–22	A group or series of four
22–23	Sped
23–24	Finer point
24–25	Accountable
25–26	Arm joints
26–27	Faints
27–28	Made snorting sound while asleep
28–29	Ridicule
29–30	Person in charge of a newspaper
30–31	Putrid or decaying
31–32	Caught
32–33	Hold in custody
33–34	Another name for nicotinic acid
34–35	US or Canadian coin worth five cents

The grid (with example filled in):

1 B	O	I		L	E	2 D
3 D	E	V				4
5						6

(grid continues with numbered cells 5 through 35)

A to Z

Fill in the missing letters of the following thirteen words with the aid of the clues:

$$--A--B--$$
Achievable

$$--C-D----$$
Trees which shed their leaves annually

$$--E-F--$$
French army officer imprisoned on Devil's Island

$$--G--H--$$
In conjunction

$$-I-J-$$
Famous turtles

$$--K-L$$
Simple country-dweller

$$---M-N---$$
County of Northern Ireland

$$-O---P-$$
Crooked

$$-Q-----R$$
Leveller

$$--S--T--$$
Russian mystic

$$-U----V-$$
Inflicting punishment

$$----W-X$$
Material used in polishes

$$--Y--Z-$$
Give a conventional form to

FIGHT AND PLAY

Each of the following 20 word combinations rhymes with a well-known phrase. For example, 'fight and play' rhymes with the phrase 'night and day'. Can you work out the phrases?

1. Gong and glance
2. Stencil and caper
3. Floods and battles
4. Chart and bowl
5. Sieve and bake
6. Fate and flee
7. Silk and daughter
8. Fleet and Friday
9. Stuck and strive
10. Whim and whopper
11. Draw and crease
12. Pine and candy
13. Tinned and main
14. Flag and groan
15. Quick and ran
16. Gun and flames
17. Jack and crew
18. Drip and pride
19. Fin and chronic
20. Slack and shrill

CONSONANTS

Insert each of the following consonants to complete the crossword:

T P L S P V G N

M L R N T R S L

L P L T R S C

CRYPTOGRAMS

Each puzzle consists of one cryptic clue. The answer is an anagram found within the clue.

1. **CHANGED MAID ONCE JUST TO RAISE A LAUGH** (8)	2. **HOODLUM REPAIRS SPEED ROAD** (9)
3. **TOM'S TRAIN SEAT REARRANGED FOR THE MAN IN CHARGE** (13)	4. **DREAM LILT MONOTONOUS EVEN WHEN GIVEN NEW ARRANGEMENT** (9)
5. **KILLERS RENT ROME TAXIS IN CONFUSION** (13)	6. **APE'S RAID SPOILED DIVINE ABODE** (8)

ANAGRAM JOURNEY

The following are all anagrams of towns and cities lying between the South coast of England and Scotland:

1. RUM HOTPOTS	7. SECOND ART
2. RECENT WISH	8. SUGAR BROOCH
3. RIDE NAG	9. HEATED GAS
4. SORE LEG CUT	10. SWEET CLAN
5. NOVEL WORM PATH	11. INK CLAW
6. GIANT MONTH	12. HINDER BUG

'DOUS'

Only four commonly used words in the English language end in 'DOUS'. Can you name them?

MAGIC WORD SQUARE

The answers to the five clues are all five-letter words which, when placed correctly in the grid, will form a magic word square where all five words can be read both across and down.

CLUES (in no particular order)

Former England cricket captain

Mark used to indicate the place in written or printed matter where something is to be inserted.

Spells

Girl's name meaning peace

The public square of an ancient Greek town

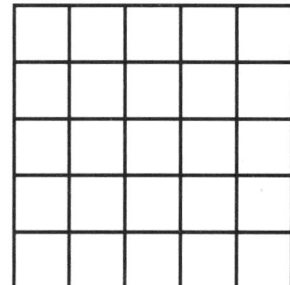

BODY PARTS

Apart from slang words, there are only ten parts of the body that are spelled with three letters. One of these is JAW. Use each of the remaining nine body parts once only to complete the following words:

LE – – – E

H – – – T

K – – – D

MOT – – – S

B – – – E

E – – – ANT

CA – – – ER

CH – – – ING

WORS – – –

SCRABBLE

1. What are the two longest words that can be made from the letters
NETIADRTMA

2. What are the two longest words that can be made from the letters
XEIOTHOSPE

3. What is the longest word that can be made from the letters
REDLEWPVFA

4. What are the four longest words that can be made from the letters
SQUPOMSMRE

5. What are the two longest words that can be made from the letters
GIELSBUAEL

6. What is the longest word that can be made from the letters
CROIAEMTDP

WORD MENAGERIE

Reading downwards, insert the name of a creature in each box to complete the list of three-letter words. No three-letter words are repeated in the eight puzzles.

❶

JA (–)
PE (–)
EN (–)
LE (–)
CU (–)
FU (–)

❷

EL (–)
RU (–)
FA (–)
MA (–)
SE (–)
DO (–)

❸

RI (–)
TE (–)
FE (–)
TO (–)
AI (–)
PA (–)
FO (–)

❹

TA (–)
SK (–)
TA (–)
SP (–)
OA (–)
OF (–)
BE (–)

❺

ER (–)
BA (–)
CA (–)
LI (–)
AL (–)
AG (–)
CA (–)
SU (–)

❻

AC (–)
IL (–)
HO (–)
LA (–)
AS (–)
LE (–)
PA (–)
HA (–)

❼

HA (–)
TO (–)
FA (–)
WO (–)
DU (–)
DA (–)

❽

AW (–)
PI (–)
WH (–)
DI (–)
BO (–)
BA (–)
FE (–)

COMPUTER THEME CROSSWORD

All answers are computer terms:

CLUES

Across

1. Software that allows calculations in ledger format
5. Small portable computer
7. The symbols, characters and numbers enabling you to communicate with the computer
9. Symbol appearing on the screen to indicate computer files
10. The physical and mechanical components of a computer system
11. The system of computer networks in which on-line communication takes place
13. To start up a program
14. A computer device or series of devices that store information
15. Equal to 1,048,576 bytes

Down

2. Letters and numbers
3. Collection of interconnecting networks
4. The cause of an unexpected malfunction
6. A device that connects a computer with a peripheral
8. A list of files stored in a computer
12. Eight bits
13. The smallest piece of computer information

CAPITALS

Move horizontally and vertically – but not diagonally – from square to adjoining square to spell out 21 capital cities. It doesn't matter which city you identify first as providing you make the correct turnings you will eventually travel through each of the 144 squares and return to a square adjacent to your starting point.

H	K	C	S	W	R	A	W	I	L	W	O
O	L	O	T	A	S	O	N	S	B	O	C
D	M	I	N	O	N	D	K	O	T	N	S
U	B	L	C	L	T	O	Y	G	K	O	O
O	R	I	A	E	S	B	A	N	B	K	M
C	O	P	E	R	A	H	G	L	E	G	O
N	E	G	N	B	U	C	R	N	S	A	I
V	I	A	H	O	B	M	A	O	A	N	T
N	E	E	L	S	L	O	D	T	G	N	I
N	D	H	N	I	O	C	E	O	S	L	H
A	I	R	K	I	C	I	A	S	O	O	S
M	A	D	I	N	O	S	L	A	G	W	A

15

DIRECTIONAL CROSSWORD

All answers travel in the direction of a compass point and start and finish in one of the shaded squares

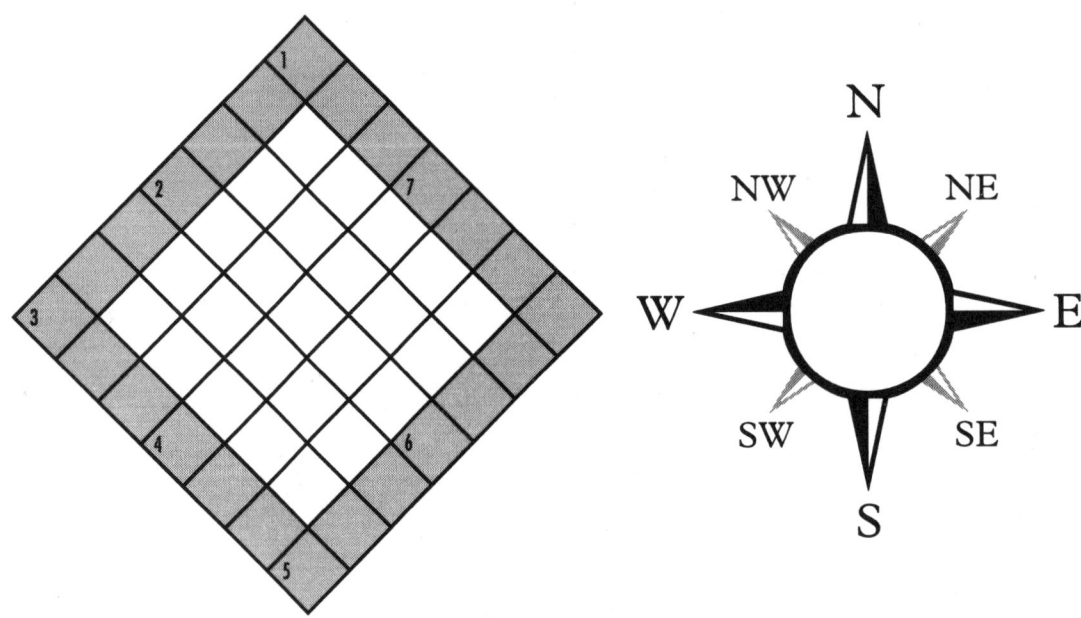

CLUES

1 SW   Garments or clothing
1 S   Friendly
1 SE   Be in anguish
2 S   Slightly open
3 E   Adorable
4 NE   Captured again
5 NE   Overshadow

5 NW   Everlasting
6 NW   The daughter of a Spanish king
6 W   —— Stravinsky
6 N   Type of metal
7 W   Star that undergoes an explosion and suddenly brightens

CROSSWORD SEARCH

Find **24** words in the bottom grid that will fit into the top crossword grid.
The words in the bottom grid can be found horizontally, vertically or diagonally, backwards
or forwards, but always in a straight line.

17

SEVEN AGES

Complete the seven words with the aid of the clues provided.

AGE – – – – – –   Generation divisions (3-6)

– AGE – – – –   Spectacular display

– – AGE – – – –   Theatre entrance (5-4)

– – – AGE – – –   Collection of animals

– – – – AGE – –   Type of British shopkeeper

– – – – – AGE –   Plan to deceive an enemy

– – – – – – AGE   Spying

KNICKERBOCKER GLORIES

Which three of the following are *not* anagrams of **KNICKERBOCKER GLORIES**?

KING SORCERER BIKE-LOCK

BLOKE KICKING SORCERER

BLOCKING KICK SEE ERROR

CRINGES LIKE CORK BROKE

GIRLIE BROKE CORKS NECK

GROCER LIKES KEEN BRICK

CORKING LIKE BEER CORKS

RISK REBLOCKING COOKER

BERSERK KICKING COOLER

LINK SICK BROKEN GROCER

BROKE GIRLS KICK ENCORE

KEENER GIRL COOKS BRICK

GROCERS BROKE LINE KICK

CORKING BEERS LIKE ROCK

ANAGRAM PHRASES

Each of the following is an anagram of a well-known phrase. Can you solve them with the help of the clues?

I. HID TO EARTH

Clue: Set the wheels in motion

2. SO DATE ALONE

Clue: Just kicking around

3. THE BORED AFFAIRS

Clue: Stick together

4. A PERFECT ECHO

Clue: Make all the running

5. MANAGE FUNDS

Clue: What this book is about

6. NINE RADISHES

Clue: Time for breakfast!

CRYPTIC CROSSWORD

CLUES

Across

1. Find fault in California for a possible shake-up (10)
8. Strange sighting on Beaufort Scale (3)
9. Ravel net in apposite fashion (8)
10. Some scope to make musical drama with rapid start (5)
11. Nip back to social dance and find amusement machine (7)
12. Award for early US President (5)
15. Ride around North to find appropriate eating place (5)
18. Consolation brings limited sympathy when cold (7)
19. Brusque among strange trees (5)
21. Begin with commanding officer and two thousand at the outset (8)
23. Leguminous plant baffles ape (3)
24. No rash lies to organize largest portion (5, 5)

Down

2. Of high quality, in or out of the pack (3)
3. Shiver, with cold or fear (7)
4. Sounds like a game bird for Dan the Potato Man (6)
5. Out to disassemble a small vehicle (4)
6. Exclamation of triumph at bathtime (6)
7. Bring back roster somewhat dictatorially (4)
9. Swift part of a river (5)
13. Revive or renovate (7)
14. Heading for a championship (5)
16. Is it conventional for Cheers favourite to visit Alcatraz, albeit briefly (6)
17. Cultivated tropical American herb in universe (6)
19. Measuring strip (4)
20. Repetition when Greek nymph arranges some chores (4)
22. Return carriage in crack condition (3)

REBUSES

Each of the following represents a familiar phrase.

CUBIC JIG WORD

Each cube shows three faces. Only one face on each of the nine cubes will fit correctly into the grid. Select the nine correct faces and fit them into the grid to form a symmetrical crossword.

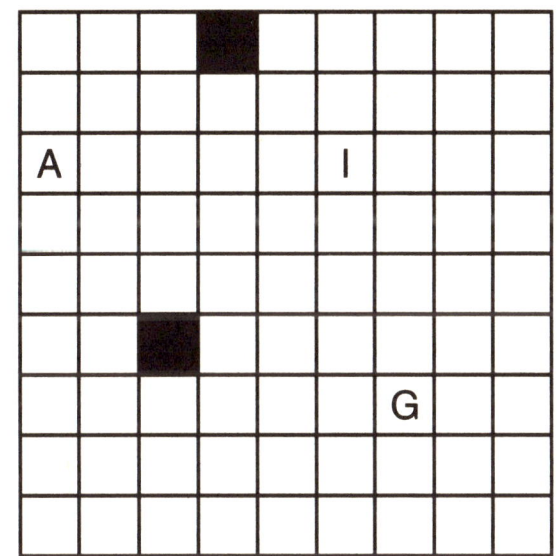

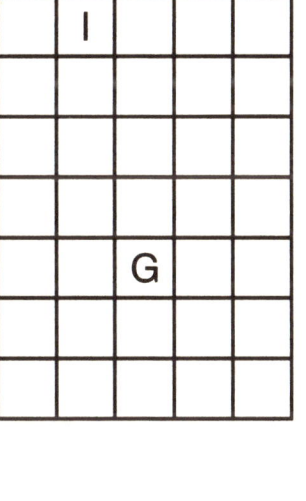

anagram crossword

Answers are anagrams of the clues.

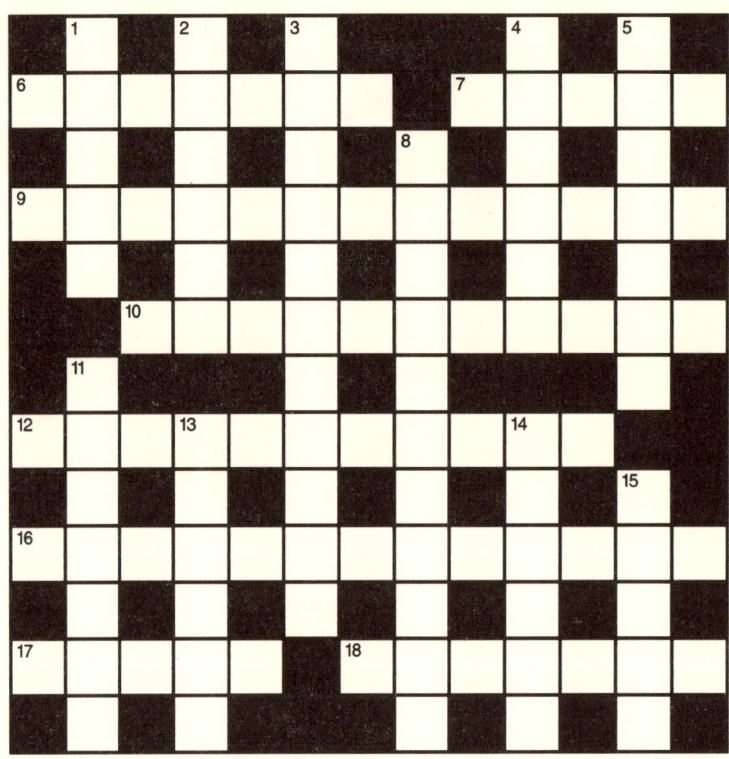

CLUES

Across

6. SLAP OAR
7. OGLED
9. TRANSMIT RADIO
10. BEAN IS PALER
12. GREETS PILOT
16. SNEERING ANTIC
17. I LEAD
18. AIR BANG

Down

1. AN PAD
2. TO RAIN
3. IGNORE DENIM
4. O SATAN
5. GLIB ONE
8. TAG ARTICLES
11. TO ADORN
13. ANT RAT
14. ED'S LEG
15. I CARD

TREASURE ISLAND

Here is a treasure island. Can you decipher the grid to find where the treasure is buried?

T	H	H	E	E	T	T	H
R	I	E	R	A	D	S	R
U	O	R	W	E	A	I	N
S	D	I	D	N	O	T	W
H	N	E	T	A	H	R	E
E	F	A	O	L	U	O	R
C	T	A	H	T	C	E	O
D	L	O	U	N	M	T	N

UNIQUE TRIGRAMS

A trigram is a set of three letters which appear adjacent in a word. For example, the word TRIGRAM itself contains the trigrams TRI, RIG, IGR, GRA and RAM. Several trigrams are unique to just one word – for example, the trigram WKW is unique to the word AWKWARD, not counting of course derivations of the same word, such as AWKWARDNESS. Below is a list of trigrams that are each unique to one word only.
All the words are in common usage.
What are they?

ADQ	GZA	SIQ
DPH	HYX	SPB
EKD	KSG	SYG
EZV	LLJ	WDU
FSP	LTD	XGL
GNP	OKC	XTD
GNT	PEV	ZWO

DOUBLET

Change GRASS to GREEN in 8 steps

```
G R A S S
_ _ _ _ _
_ _ _ _ _
_ _ _ _ _
_ _ _ _ _
_ _ _ _ _
_ _ _ _ _
_ _ _ _ _
G R E E N
```

Complete the seven words with the aid of the clues provided.

SIN – – – – – –   Republic of SE Asia

– SIN – – – – –   Another name for mica

– – SIN – – – –   Rid of harmful microorganisms

– – – SIN – – –   With humour

– – – – SIN – –   Former name of Ethiopia

– – – – – SIN –   Bewildering

– – – – – – SIN   State of USA, capital Madison

SELECT-A-LETTER CROSSWORD

The clues are given, but as an additional aid you can select the correct letter from a choice of three or four letters in each square.

CLUES

Across

3. Edged (9)
8. Sound like an ass (4)
9. Strange (10)
10. Loose rope (4)
11. Successor (4)
13. Go in (5)
17. Laze about (6)
18. Parrots (6)
19. Two in cards (5)
22. Incite (4)
24. Pain (4)
25. Translucent (10)
26. Formerly (4)
27. Sent (8)

Down

1. Fishing gear (5)
2. Type of orchestra (9)
4. Animal (5)
5. Funeral song (5)
6. Chicken's perch (5)
7. Trouble (8)
12. Animal (4)
14. Having a nucleus (8)
15. Flowers (8)
16. Ruler (4)
20. Disarm (5)
21. Put pressure upon (5)
22. Relative (5)
23. Board game (5)

GRANDFATHER

'My grandfather was eight years old on his first birthday,' said the boy. How was that?

BIRTHDAY

I wished to know the birthday of my secretary. I knew it was in February, and the year was 2000, but which day? I asked six office colleagues who each gave me a cryptic clue:

A said 'It's an odd number'
B said 'It's a prime number'
C said 'It's a single digit'
D said 'It's a double digit'
E said 'It has at least one 2 in it'
F said 'It's between 25 and 29'

I knew that one of them had lied. What was the date? (1 is not considered to be a prime number)

BROKEN WINDOW

One day a window was found broken in the house where Arthur, Bill and Charlie lived. When questioned by their father these were their answers, but at least one of the statements was true and at least one was false. Who broke the window?

Arthur: 'Bill did not break the window'

Bill: 'I did not break the window'

Charlie: 'I broke the window'

LANGUAGES

At a college there were 100 students:

38 studied Latin
32 studied French
24 studied German
17 studied Latin and French
13 studied French and German
11 studied Latin and German
6 studied all three languages

How many studied none of these?

WIN

26 cards, each featuring a different letter of the alphabet are placed face down on a table. What are the chances that, when *three* are turned up at random, the cards will spell WIN?

MULTIGRAMS

Find 10 words using only the letters shown, any of which may be used more than once. The number of letters in each word is given in brackets.
Example: ABN (6) = BANANA

1. DOV (6)

2. BEJU (6)

3. DOH (6)

4. LAF (7)

5. APIZ (7)

6. ABHORU (8)

7. EPRSX (9)

8. BEKOPR (10)

9. EHLNPS (12)

10. ELNPS (13)

SAFE

A four-letter word will open the safe. Revolve the letters to the square window to find the word.

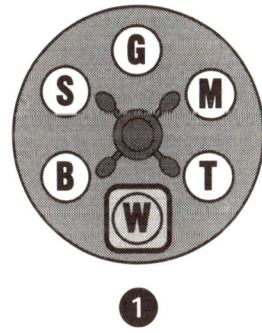

1

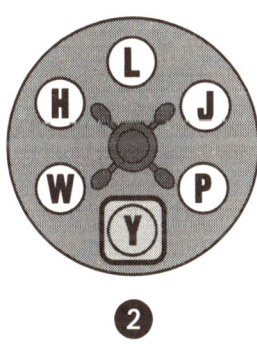

2

3

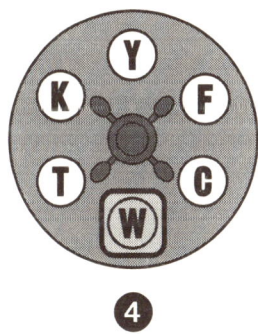

4

PALINDROMES

The earliest documented palindrome in the English language, published in 1614, is

LEWD DID I LIVE, EVIL I DID DWEL

Can you solve the following palindromes:

1. N – – S –, I S – Y, G – – S – – S, R – –
2. N – – G – – –, O, R – – R, A – – – N

DECIMATE

When the Roman army needed to punish a large number of men, every tenth soldier was executed – hence the word 'decimate'. Imagine you are one of 1000 mutinous pirates who have been captured and tied to numbered posts arranged in a circle. The first pirate is to be executed followed by every alternate pirate until only one, who will be set free, remains. Which numbered post would you choose?

DE MERE'S PROBLEM

Several hundred years ago, gaming houses would offer odds of even money that a gambler would throw at least one six in four throws of a standard die. What are the true odds?

BRACKETS

Find a word which, when placed at the end of the first word, makes a new word; and, when placed in front of the second word, makes another new word.

CHIMNEY (– – – – –) STAKE

PENNY (– – – – –) BERRY

WATER (– – – – –) BARROW

BAND (– – – – –) TRAIN

DEAD (– – – –) SMITH

DAISY (– – – – –) GANG

POWDER (– – – –) ADDER

BUSH (– – – –) ALARM

CHARM (– – – – – –) BOY

HOCKEY

A hockey team of eleven players is to be selected from 8 boys and 7 girls. There are to be 6 boys and 5 girls in the team. How many different teams are possible?

CIRCLES

Which circle should replace the one with a question mark?

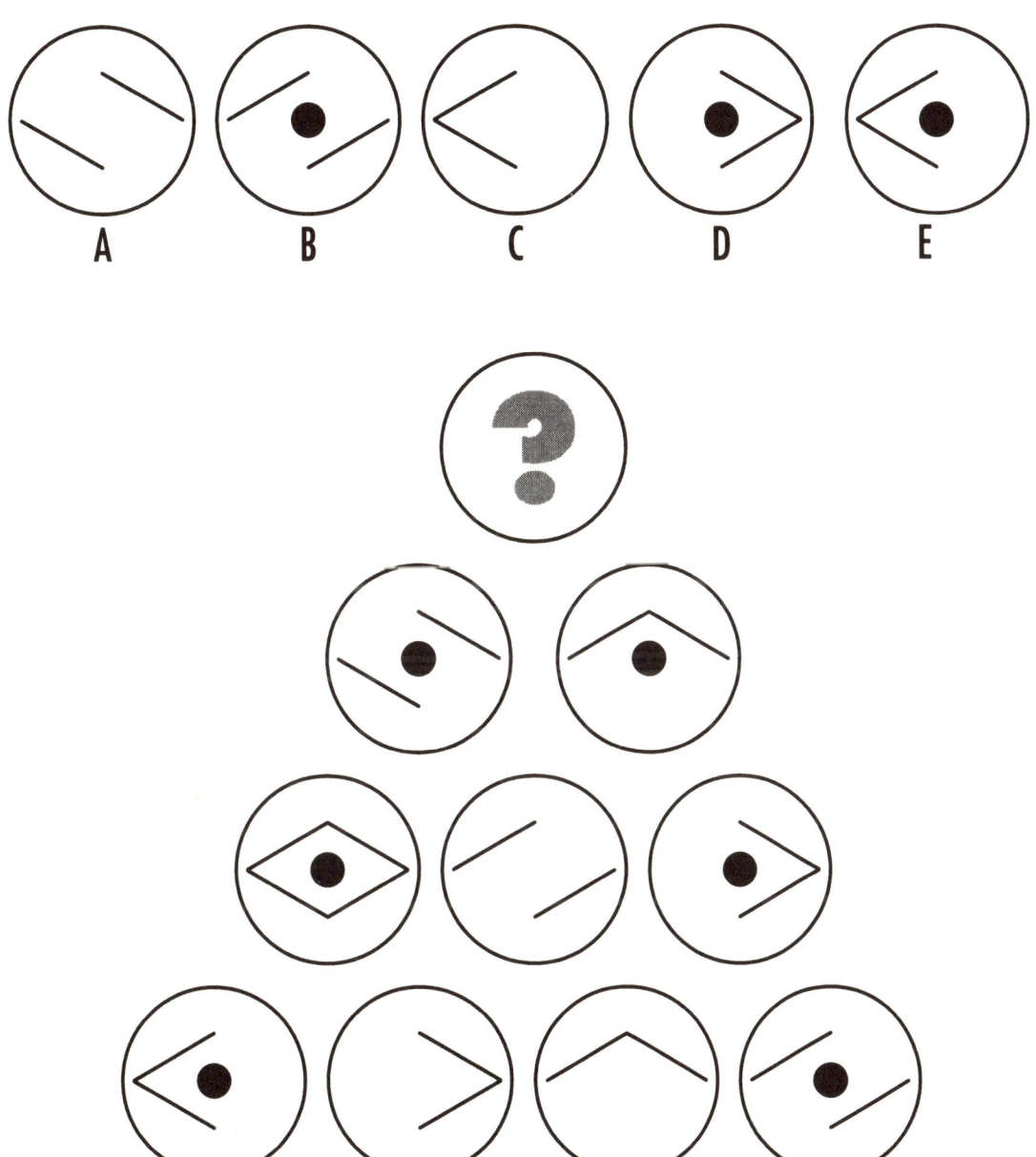

ONE-ARMED BANDIT

Nudge the buttons up or down to change PATRICK into another boys' name.
(Four letters do not need to be changed)

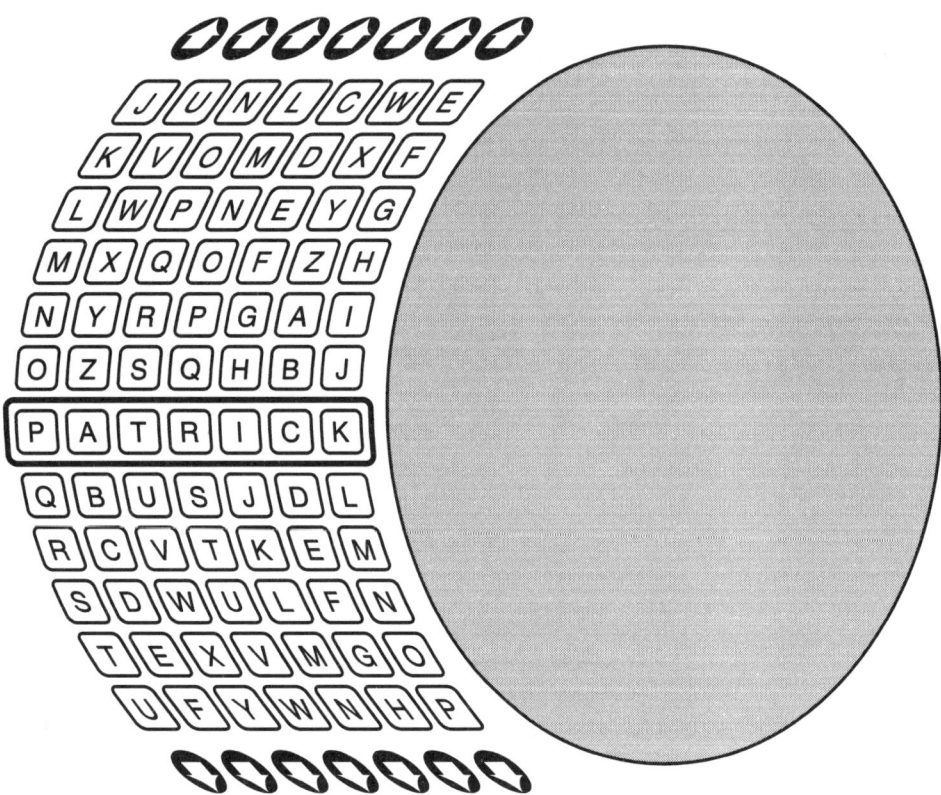

LOGIC

From the information given below, and by filling in the chart, can you work out the age and occupation of each man and where he came from?

Mr Smith came from Birmingham and was not aged 40
The man from Glasgow was a builder aged 40
Mr Jones was a builder and did not come from London
The accountant was not aged 30
Mr Smith was not the driver

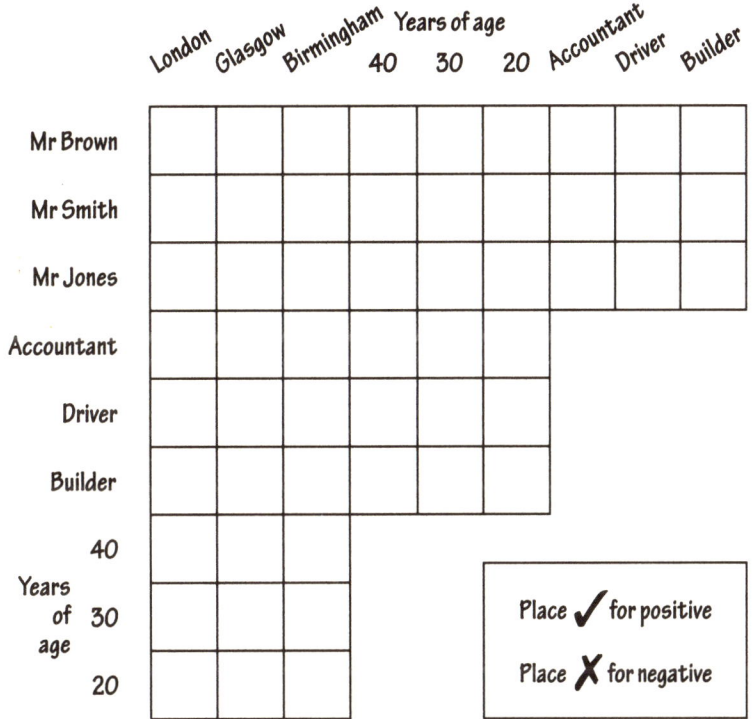

Place ✓ for positive

Place ✗ for negative

EIGHTS

Solve the eight clues.

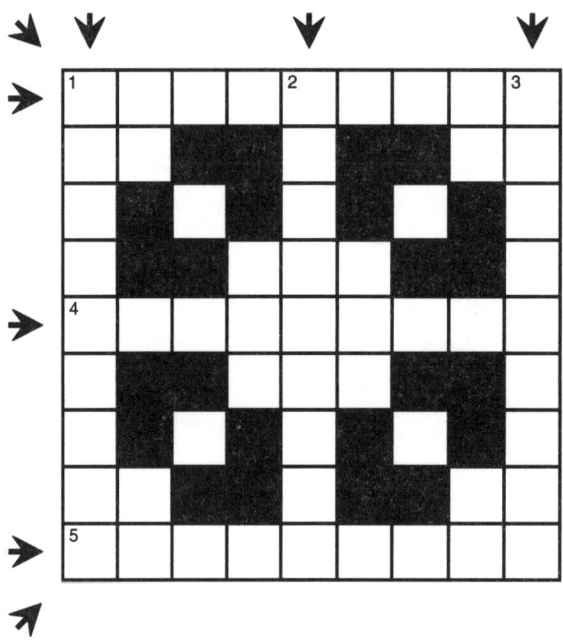

CLUES

Across
1. Chinese officials
4. Landlord
5. Gives out medicine

Diagonal
1. Spies use these
5. Objects thrown away

Down
1. Disfigured
2. Instrument for astronomy
3. Astonishes

PYRAMID

Spell out a ten-letter word by entering the rooms. Each room may be entered only once, but you may go into the passageway as many times as you wish.

CLUE: Outward look

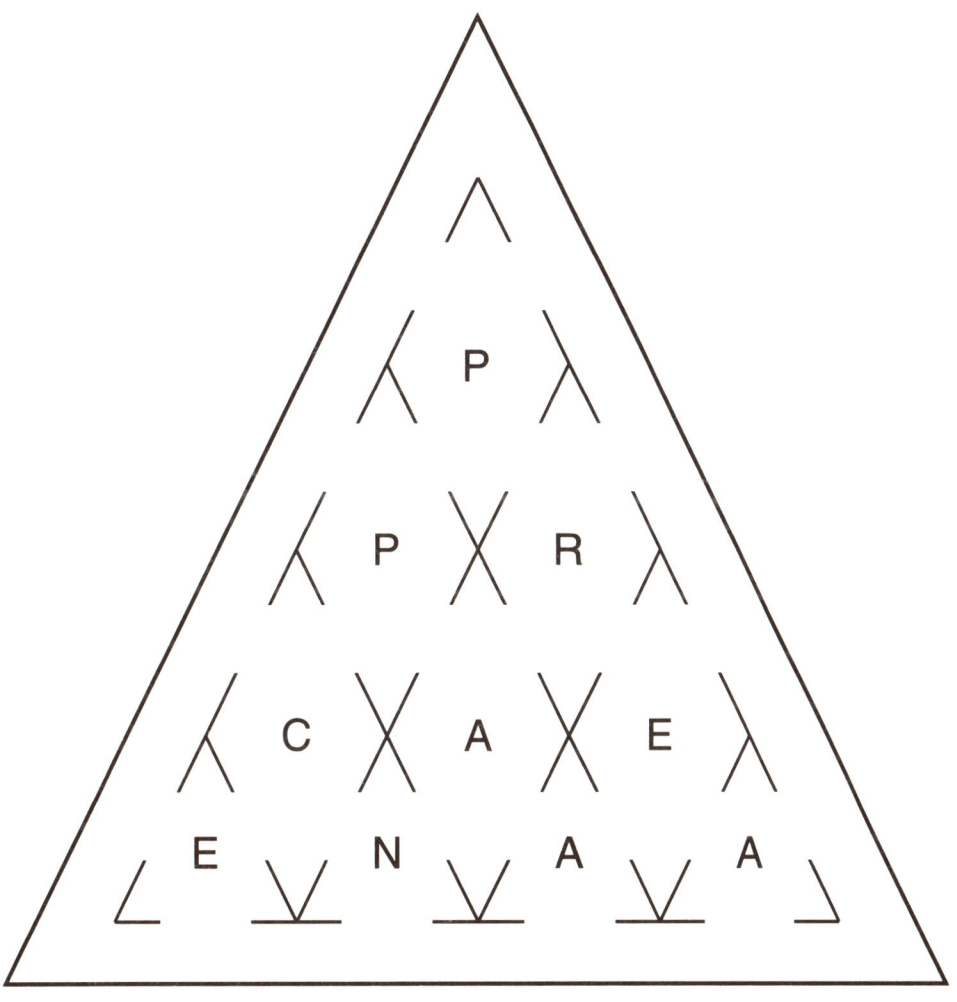

HONEYCOMB

Find 16 fruits using adjacent letters. You can double a letter or use the same letter more than once in each word.

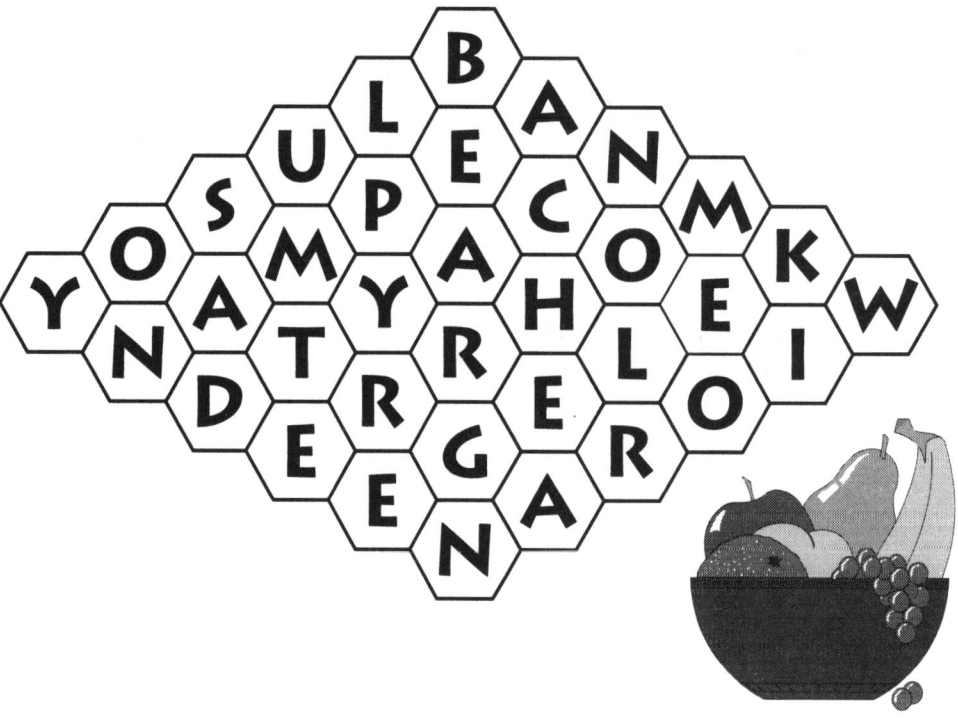

DOUBLE REBUS

Find the pairs of rebuses that will make up two occupations.

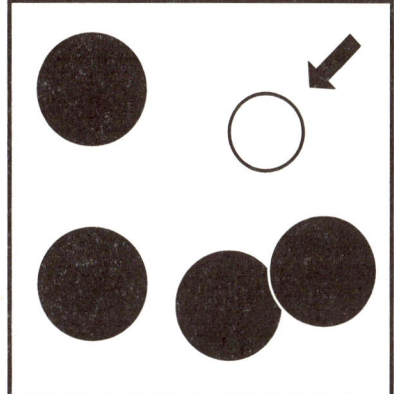

CRICKET

A consignment of new cricket bats arrived at the ground. 19 team members were allocated new bats as follows:

No 1 Batsman was given $\frac{1}{19}$ of the consignment plus $\frac{1}{19}$ of a bat

No 2 Batsman was given $\frac{1}{18}$ of the consignment plus $\frac{1}{18}$ of a bat

and so on until

the last but one was given $\frac{1}{2}$ of the remainder plus $\frac{1}{2}$ of a bat.

The last player was given the remainder, and immediately resigned from the club.

Why did he resign, and how many bats were delivered?

MAGIC SQUARE

Place the letters in the square so that the words read the same across and down.

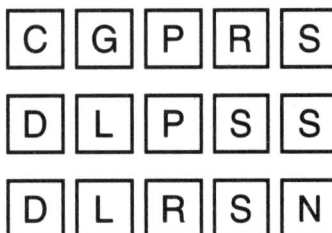

DICE

Which of the opened-out cubes A, B, C, D will fold to make the completed cube E?

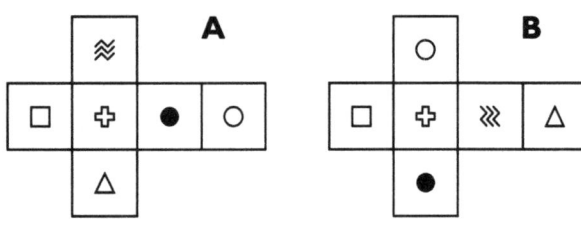

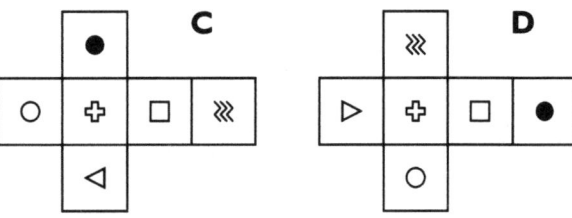

GROUPS

Which of these four groups is the odd one out?

1. Salmon, Herring, Octopus, Anchovy, Ling

2. Primrose, Orchid, Salvia, Yarrow

3. Finch, Linnet, Osprey, Cuckoo, Kingfisher

4. Lion, Elephant, Ass, Squirrel, Tiger

ALPHABET CROSSWORD

Some tiles have already been positioned, but complete the crossword grid
with the remaining alphabet tiles.

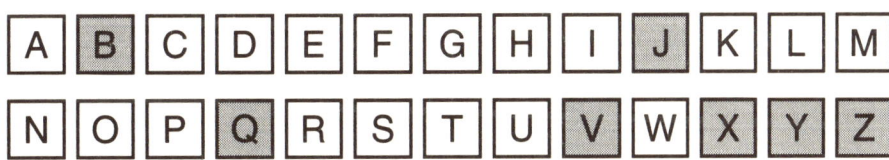

Start at the centre square and move horizontally, vertically and diagonally from square to square to spell out the names of eight card games, finishing in the top right hand square. Each square in the grid may only be used once.

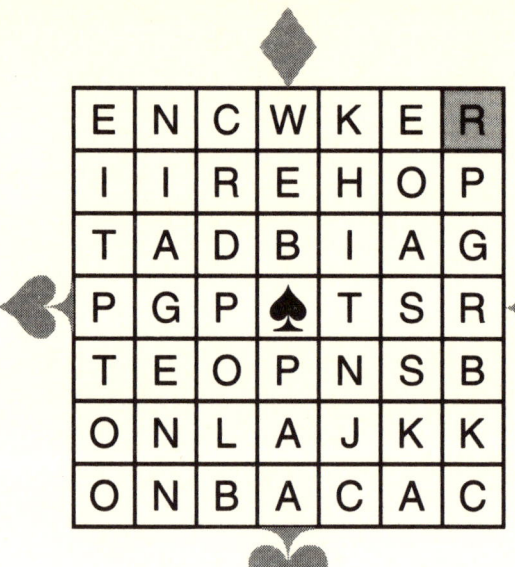

E	N	C	W	K	E	R
I	I	R	E	H	O	P
T	A	D	B	I	A	G
P	G	P	♠	T	S	R
T	E	O	P	N	S	B
O	N	L	A	J	K	K
O	N	B	A	C	A	C

GROUPS

H	E	E	L	G	G	A	G
T	D	Y	A	N	E	A	N
R	I	N	I	E	M	E	I
A	R	R	T	B	R	G	D
E	P	U	O	R	T	N	L
S	O	L	A	I	A	A	I
R	D	W	O	T	U	G	U
D	R	O	S	D	N	A	B

Hidden in this grid are 15 names of groups of Animals, Birds, Fish and People etc. Words are to be found in straight lines, forwards, backwards or diagonally.

1. Group of rooks
2. Group of geese
3. Group of machine guns
4. Group of rabbits
5. Group of musicians
6. Group of acrobats
7. Group of teal
8. Group of lambs
9. Group of whales
10. Group of lions
11. Group of pheasant
12. Group of foxes
13. Group of mallard
14. Group of elks
15. Group of wolves

DIAMOND

Words may run in any direction following the compass points.

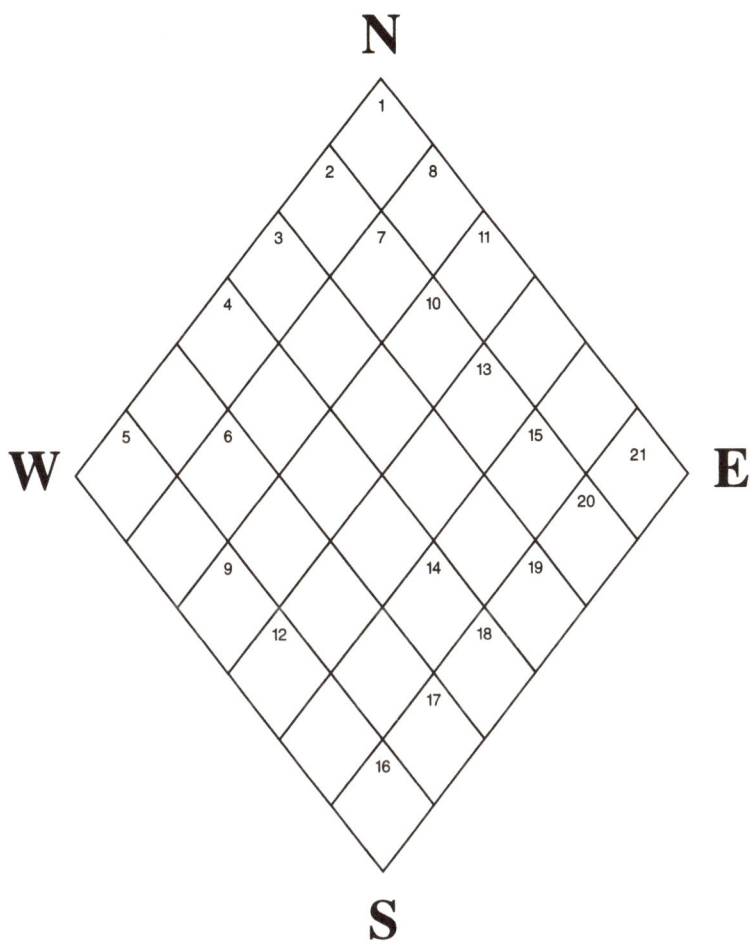

N

W

E

S

CLUES

1 SW	Racket strings	**6 SE**	Delight in	**14 N**	Many
1 SE	Animals	**7 S**	Hoar frosts	**15 W**	Destitute
1 S	Felonies	**8 S**	Small island	**16 N**	Half
2 S	Upwards	**9 NW**	Illustrations	**17 NW**	Fulcrum
3 S	Played off	**10 S**	Charge	**18 W**	Shown way
4 SW	Part of the body	**10 SE**	A light knock	**19 SW**	Ailments
5 SE	Deals	**11 S**	Post	**20 SW**	Cultivates soil
5 E	Soldiers	**12 NW**	Weapon	**21 SW**	Non-moving pictures
5 NE	Pull	**13 S**	Be ill	**21 W**	Scent

HONEYCOMB

Find 12 flowers by moving in any direction to adjacent squares.
You can double a letter or use the same letter more than once in each word.

FIVES

Place the five-letter words in the grid to complete the crossword.

LYRIC	CLIMB
SCENE	CATCH
COPES	STORE
EXTRA	BELLE
ROOMS	MUTED
ATTAR	YUCCA
AORTA	VALES
RANGE	ASPEN
PEDAL	STONE
LANES	VALET
SOTTO	COMIC
MINOR	TESTY
SLAVE	RISEN
ENNUI	TROOP
LIMBO	VOMIT
CILLA	TOTAL
SMILE	SURLY
INDIA	HYDRA

NO BLANKS

In this crossword puzzle, all the blanks have been replaced by letters.
You have to find the blanks, to produce the symmetrical puzzle.

A	S	E	M	E	S	T	E	R	S	A	C	K
S	T	R	A	I	T	S	I	P	E	T	A	L
D	A	I	N	T	Y	U	R	E	X	T	R	A
E	M	I	T	S	R	G	E	S	T	U	R	E
F	P	O	L	E	S	A	T	A	E	N	I	A
E	N	D	E	S	T	R	U	C	T	I	O	N
R	E	D	B	O	R	E	R	E	I	G	N	N
E	X	P	E	R	I	E	N	C	E	D	E	U
D	P	U	R	S	N	V	S	I	N	G	S	L
R	U	M	M	A	G	E	U	E	D	I	T	S
E	N	P	I	T	S	U	M	P	U	B	O	A
A	G	O	N	Y	A	P	A	T	R	O	N	S
M	E	T	E	R	E	D	T	H	E	R	E	H

STEPS

Place the twenty words in the crossword grid so that each horizontal and vertical line forms a word.
(Some words will share the same letter on the completed grid)

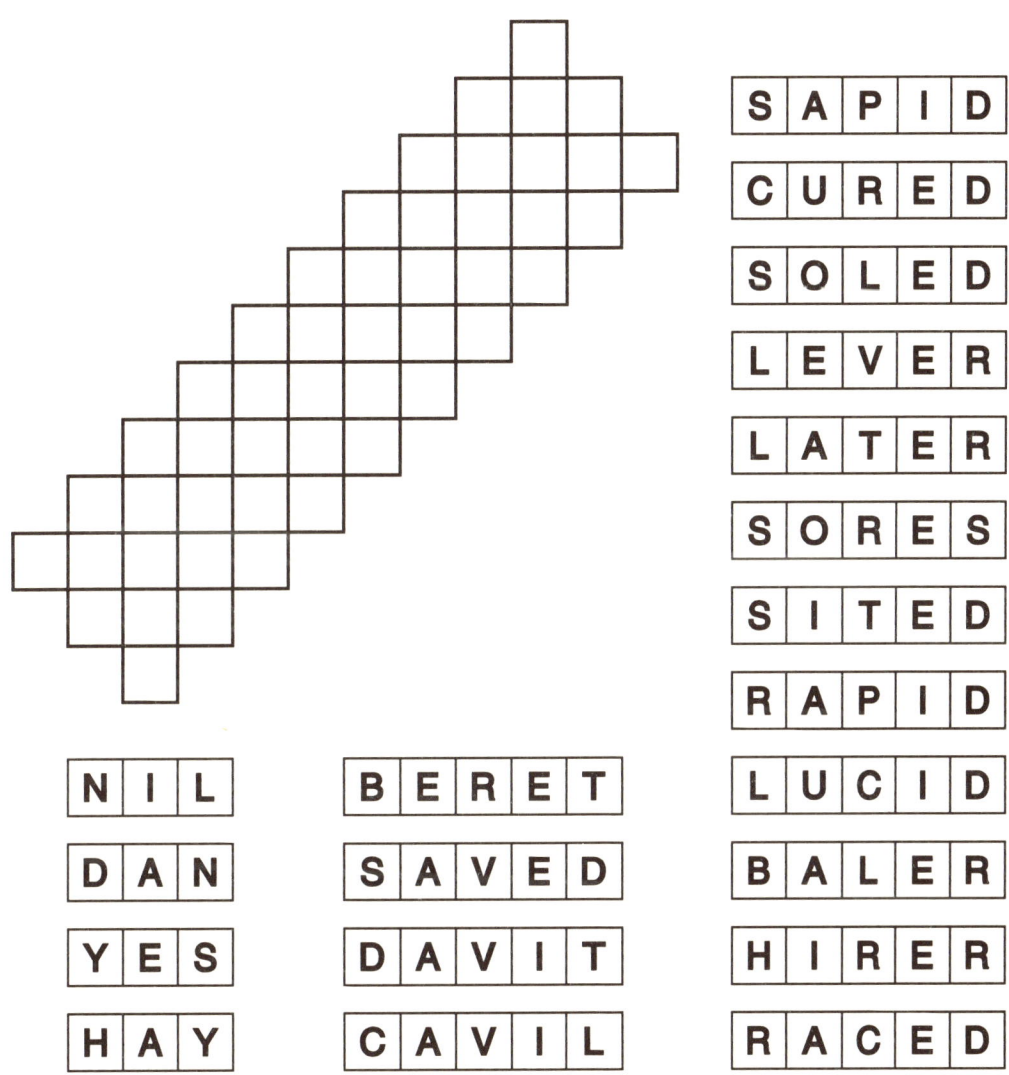

S	A	P	I	D
C	U	R	E	D
S	O	L	E	D
L	E	V	E	R
L	A	T	E	R
S	O	R	E	S
S	I	T	E	D
R	A	P	I	D
L	U	C	I	D
B	A	L	E	R
H	I	R	E	R
R	A	C	E	D

N	I	L
D	A	N
Y	E	S
H	A	Y

B	E	R	E	T
S	A	V	E	D
D	A	V	I	T
C	A	V	I	L

Vegetables *page 5*

ARTICHOKE
ASPARAGUS
AUBERGINE
MARROWFAT
Key Anagram: MANGETOUT

Paul's Age *page 6*

It was 1990 BC and 1995 BC.

Oronyms *page 6*

1. A nice man; An ice man
2. Great ape; Grey tape
3. Grade A; Grey day
4. I scream; Ice cream
5. May cough; Make off
6. Night rate; Nitrate
7. Plum pie; Plump eye
8. Slide rule; Sly drool
9. Tulips; Two lips
10. Twenty-six ones; Twenty sick swans
11. Damn pegs; Damp eggs
12. I stink; Iced ink

All Change *page 6*

1. Have a dig at
2. To fork out
3. And so forth
4. At a loose end
5. Dead set
6. Head over heels
7. To lay down the law
8. In two minds
9. Nuts and bolts
10. Top of the pops
11. Port of call

12. Take as read
13. Real life
14. To even up
15. To fall flat
16. Ill at ease
17. To come to light
18. Now and then
19. On the rack
20. To go to sea

Something in Common *page 6*

With the first letter removed, each still forms a word:

MOTIONLESS
ASTRONOMICALLY
INDICATION
LITHESOME
REASONABLENESS
EVOLUTIONARY

Magic Cube *page 7*

Vehicles *page 8*

LAND ROVER
SPORTS CAR
LIMOUSINE
BUBBLE CAR
Key Anagram: AMBULANCE

Threesomes *page 9*

1. Brown, orange, indigo
2. Tango, waltz, rumba
3. Tennis, archery, golf
4. Ottawa, Madrid, Athens
5. Giraffe, lion, elephant

Backwards and Forwards
page 9

A to Z *page 10*

feasible, deciduous, Dreyfus, together, Ninja, yokel, Fermanagh, corrupt, equaliser, Rasputin, punitive, beeswax, stylize

Fight and Play *page 10*

1. Song and dance
2. Pencil and paper
3. Goods and chattels
4. Heart and soul
5. Give and take
6. Wait and see
7. Milk and water
8. Neat and tidy
9. Duck and dive
10. Prim and proper
11. War and peace
12. Fine and dandy
13. Wind and rain
14. Rag and bone
15. Spick and span
16. Fun and games
17. Black and blue
18. Slip and slide
19. Gin and tonic
20. Jack and Jill

Consonants *page 11*

45

Cryptograms *page 12*

1. Comedian (maid once)
2. Desperado (speed road)
3. Stationmaster (Tom's train seat)
4. Treadmill (dream lilt)
5. Exterminators (rent Rome taxis)
6. Paradise (ape's raid)

Anagram Journey *page 12*

1. Portsmouth
2. Winchester
3. Reading
4. Gloucester
5. Wolverhampton
6. Nottingham
7. Doncaster
8. Scarborough
9. Gateshead
10. Newcastle
11. Alnwick
12. Edinburgh

'Dous' *page 12*

HAZARDOUS
HORRENDOUS
STUPENDOUS
TREMENDOUS

Magic Word Square *page 12*

M	A	G	I	C
A	G	O	R	A
G	O	W	E	R
I	R	E	N	E
C	A	R	E	T

Body Parts *page 13*

LEGUME
HEART
KEYED
MOTTOES
BRIBE
ELEGANT
CALIPER
CHARMING
WORSHIP

Scrabble *page 13*

1. marinated, attainder
2. isotope, exposit
3. wavered
4. summers, supremo, mosques, mousers
5. beguiles, legalise
6. decimator

Word Menagerie *page 13*

1. BADGER
2. FERRET
3. GAZELLE
4. GIRAFFE
5. ANTELOPE
6. ELEPHANT
7. DONKEY
8. LEOPARD

Computer Theme Crossword
page 14

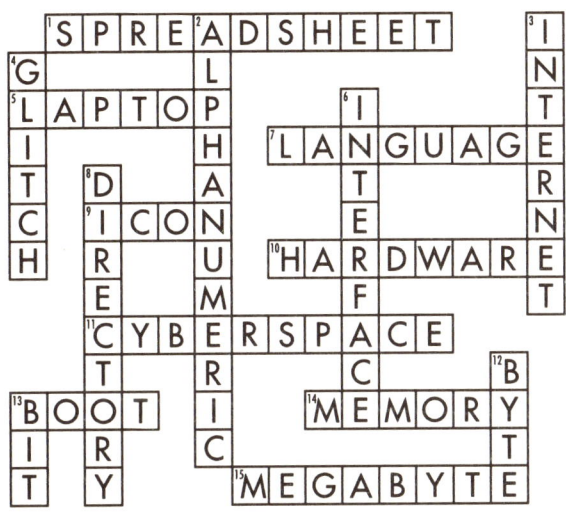

Across/Down answers shown in grid:
- SPREADSHEET
- GLITCH
- LAPTOP
- ALPHANUMERIC
- INTERNET
- DIRECTORY
- LANGUAGE
- INTERFACE
- ICON
- HARDWARE
- CYBERSPACE
- BOOT
- MEMORY
- BYTE
- MEGABYTE

Directional Crossword
page 16

Capitals
page 15

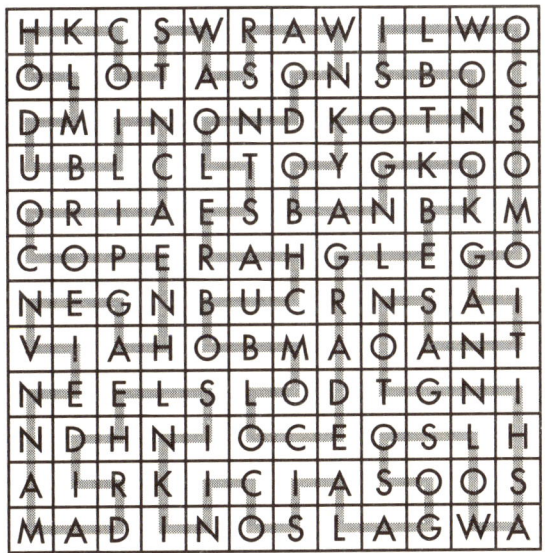

```
H K C S W R A W I L W O
O L O T A S O N S B O C
D M I N O N D K O T N S
U B L C L T O Y G K O O
O R I A E S B A N B K M
C O P E R A H G L E G O
N E G N B U C R N S A I
V I A H O B M A O A N T
N E E L S L O D T G N I
A I R K I C I A S O O S
M A D I N O S L A G W A
```

Bucharest, London, Warsaw, Stockholm, Dublin, Cairo, Copenhagen, Vienna, Madrid, Helsinki, Nicosia, Lagos, Oslo, Washington, Santiago, Moscow, Lisbon, Tokyo, Bangkok, Belgrade, Colombo.

Crossword Search
page 17

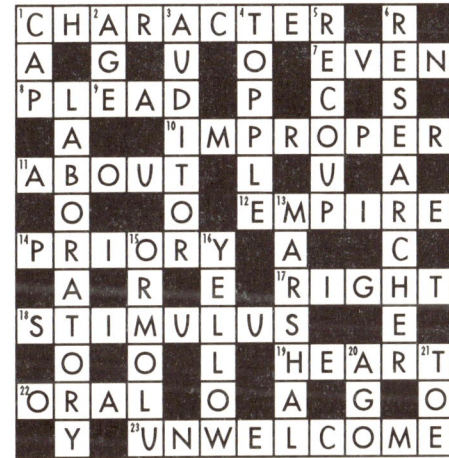

Answers in grid:
- CHARACTER
- EVEN
- PLEAD
- IMPROPER
- ABOUT
- EMPIRE
- PRIOR
- RIGHT
- STIMULUS
- HEART
- ORAL
- UNWELCOME

Seven Ages
page 18

age-groups
pageantry
stage-door
menagerie
newsagent
stratagem
espionage

Knickerbocker Glories
page 18

GROCER LIKES KEEN BRICK
RISK REBLOCKING COOKER
LINK SICK BROKEN GROCER

Anagram Phrases *page 18*

1. Hit the road
2. At a loose end
3. Birds of a feather
4. Force the pace
5. Fun and games
6. Rise and shine

Cryptic Crossword *page 19*

Rebuses *page 20*

1. Once bitten, twice shy
2. Split the difference
3. Abnormal load
4. Cross-country
5. A blot on the horizon
6. Hundreds and thousands
7. On the horns of a dilemma
8. Community centre
9. Midsummer madness
10. Iron-fisted
11. More often than not
12. Rub up the wrong way

Cubic Jig Word *page 21*

Anagram Crossword *page 22*

Treasure Island *page 23*

Start at the top left-hand square and move horizontally to alternate squares line by line. When you reach the bottom, move back to the second square on the top row and continue to move to alternate squares, to spell out the message:
'The treasure is in the area located on the third row and down the fourth column.'

Unique Trigrams *page 24*

HEADQUARTERS	ZIGZAG	PHYSIQUE
HEADPHONES	ASPHYXIA	RASPBERRY
WEEKDAY	THANKSGIVING	EASYGOING
RENDEZVOUS	KILLJOY	SAWDUST
OFFSPRING	MELTDOWN	FOXGLOVE
SIGNPOST	BOOKCASE	NEXTDOOR
SOVEREIGNTY	GRAPEVINE	BUZZWORD

Doublet *page 24*

GRASS
CRASS
CRESS
TRESS
TREES
FREES
FREED
GREED
GREEN

Seven Sins *page 24*

Singapore
Isinglass
Disinfect
Amusingly
Abyssinia
Confusing
Wisconsin

Select-a-Letter Crossword
page 25

Grandfather *page 26*

He was born on 29 February 1896.
1900 was not a leap year; there wasn't a
29 February and so he didn't have a birthday.
Therefore on 29 February 1904 he had his first
birthday, even though he was 8 years old.

Birthday *page 26*

	A	B	C	D	E	F
1	✓		✓			
2		✓	✓		✓	
3	✓	✓	✓			
4			✓			
5	✓	✓	✓			
6			✓			
7	✓	✓	✓			
8			✓			
9	✓		✓			
10				✓		
11	✓	✓		✓		
12				✓	✓	
13	✓	✓		✓		
14				✓		
15	✓			✓		
16				✓		
17	✓	✓		✓		
18				✓		
19	✓	✓		✓		
20				✓	✓	
21	✓			✓	✓	
22				✓	✓	
23	✓	✓		✓	✓	
24				✓	✓	
25	✓			✓	✓	✓
26				✓	✓	✓
27	✓			✓	✓	✓
28				✓	✓	✓
29	✓	✓		✓	✓	✓

Answer: 29 – The only day with 5 ticks,
indicating 5 true answers

Broken Window *page 26*

	Arthur's Statement	Bill's Statement	Charlie's Statement
If it was Arthur	True	True	False
If it was Bill	False	False	False
If it was Charlie	True	True	True

It was Arthur who was the culprit.
If it was Bill, all statements would be false.
If it was Charlie, all statements would be true.

Languages *page 26*

This is solved by a Venn diagram:

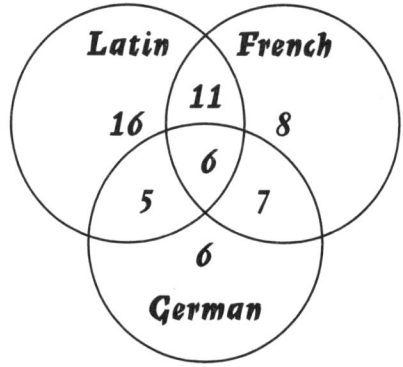

Latin 38 *minus* 22 (11 + 6 + 5)
French 32 *minus* 24 (11 + 6 + 7)
German 24 *minus* 18 (5 + 6 + 7)
16 + 11 + 5 + 6 + 8 + 7 + 6 = 59
100 *minus* 59 = 41
Therefore: 41 studied none

Win *page 26*

You have a one in 26 chance of turning over a W. When that card is turned over, 25 cards are left face down, so you have a one in 25 chance of turning over an I. Then, you have a one in 24 chance of turning over an N. To work out the chances of turning over the whole word, do the following calculation:

$$\frac{1}{26} \times \frac{1}{25} \times \frac{1}{24} = 15600$$

so 1 chance in 15600

Multigrams *page 26*

1. VOODOO
2. JUJUBE
3. HOODOO
4. ALFALFA
5. PIZZAZZ
6. BROUHAHA
7. EXPRESSES
8. BOOKKEEPER
9. HELPLESSNESS
10. SLEEPLESSNESS

Safe *page 27*

SPRY

Palindromes *page 28*

1. NURSE, I SPY, GYPSIES, RUN
2. NIAGARA, O ROAR, AGAIN

Decimate *page 28*

Take 2 to the power which gives the lowest number above 1000 which is
$$2^{10} = 1024$$

Formula $= 1024 - ((1024 - 1000) \times 2) = 976$

De Mere's Problem *page 28*

The odds that it will not happen are
$$\left(\tfrac{5}{6}\right)^4 = \cdot482$$

Therefore, the odds that it will happen are ·518
The odds favour the house

Brackets *page 28*

SWEEP
BLACK
WHEEL
WAGON
LOCK
CHAIN
PUFF
FIRE
SCHOOL

Hockey *page 28*

$$\frac{8! - 2!}{6!} \times \frac{7! - 2!}{5!}$$

$$\frac{8 \times 7 \times 6 \times 5 \times 4 \times 3}{1 \times 2 \times 3 \times 4 \times 5 \times 6} \times \frac{7 \times 6 \times 5 \times 4 \times 3}{1 \times 2 \times 3 \times 4 \times 5}$$

$$= 28 \times 21$$
$$= 588$$

Circles *page 29*

C

Each pair of circles combine to form the circle above, but similar symbols disappear.

One-Armed Bandit *page 30*

MAURICE

Logic *page 31*

Name	Place	Age	Occupation
Brown	London	30	Driver
Smith	Birmingham	20	Accountant
Jones	Glasgow	40	Builder

Eights *page 32*

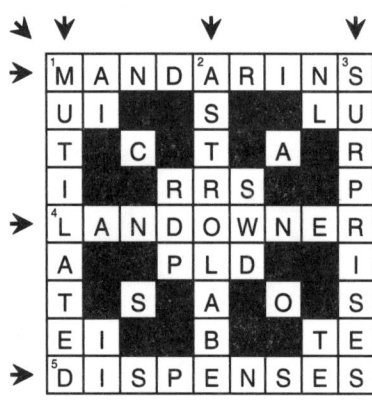

Pyramid *page 33*

APPEARANCE

Honeycomb *page 34*

PAPAYA	PEAR
PEACH	APPLE
CHERRY	BANANA
PECAN	MELON
LEMON	GRAPE
PLUM	ORANGE
KIWI	GREENGAGE
DATE	DAMSON

Double Rebus *page 35*

STEEPLE-JACK
CHIMNEY-SWEEP

Cricket *page 36*

Every batsman had 2 bats except the last who had only 1. There were 37 bats delivered, ie.

$$\frac{1}{19} \times 37 = 1\frac{18}{19} + \frac{1}{19} = 2$$

$$\frac{1}{18} \times 35 = 1\frac{17}{18} + \frac{1}{18} = 2$$

$$\frac{1}{17} \times 33 = 1\frac{16}{17} + \frac{1}{17} = 2$$

$$\frac{1}{16} \times 31 = 1\frac{15}{16} + \frac{1}{16} = 2$$

etc until penultimate batsman

$$\frac{1}{2} \times 3 = 1\frac{1}{2} + \frac{1}{2} = 2$$

Last batsman takes remainder = 1 and resigns because of unfair treatment.

Magic Square *page 36*

C	L	A	S	P
L	A	S	E	R
A	S	I	D	E
S	E	D	G	E
P	R	E	E	N

Dice *page 36*

C

Groups *page 36*

Initial letters spell out:
1. SHOAL (of fish)
2. POSY (of flowers)
3. FLOCK (of birds)
4. LEAST (odd one out)

Alphabet Crossword *page 37*

Card Games *page 38*

Bridge Patience Whist Snap Pontoon
Blackjack Brag Poker

Groups *page 38*

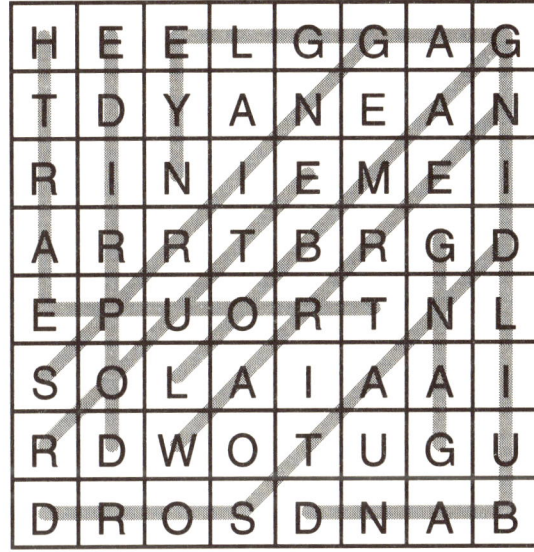

1. BUILDING
2. GAGGLE
3. STAND
4. WARREN
5. BAND
6. TROUPE
7. SPRING
8. GAMBOL
9. POD
10. PRIDE
11. NYE
12. EARTH
13. SORD
14. GANG
15. ROUTE

Diamond *page 39*

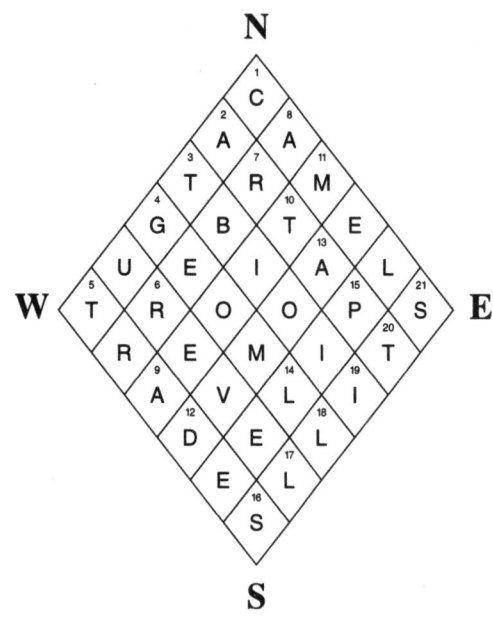

No Blanks *page 42*

Honeycomb *page 40*

DAHLIA	ZINNIA	POPPY
MIMOSA	ASTER	LILAC
CROCUS	ROSE	PEONY
DAISY	LILY	MAY

Steps *page 43*

Fives *page 41*

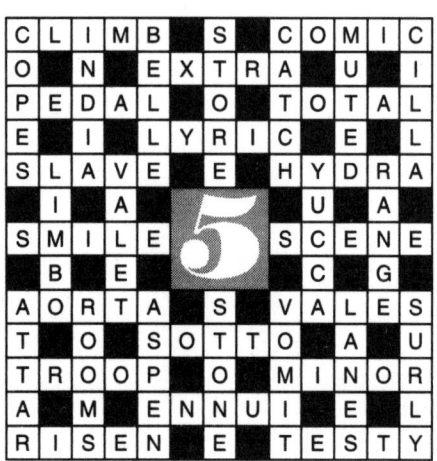

QUIZZES

NUMBERS GAME

What do the following phrases involving numbers mean? For example:

7 D S = Seven Deadly Sins

3 L on a T

4 S in a D of C

7 D in S W

8 L on a S

9 S by B

10 L I B

10 P in C

11 F in a C

11 P in a C T

12 A at the L S

14 D in a F

20 Y S by R V W

25 Y of M for a S A

30 D H S

32 D F at which W F

64 S on a C

500 S in a R

1000 S L by the F of H of T

1440 M in a D

5280 F in a M

TRIVIA MISCELLANY

1. Who was the father of James and John, two of the twelve apostles of Jesus?
- **(a)** Nathan
- **(b)** Zebedee
- **(c)** Levi
- **(d)** Zachariah

2. What was invented in 1839 in America by a West Point cadet Abner Doubleday?
- **(a)** Coca-Cola
- **(b)** Football
- **(c)** The Zipper
- **(d)** Baseball

3. The drachma is the unit of currency of which country?
- **(a)** Greece
- **(b)** Albania
- **(c)** Turkey
- **(d)** Hungary

4. Which tree produces edible fruit called persimmons?
- **(a)** Beech
- **(b)** Oak
- **(c)** Yulan
- **(d)** Ebony

5. Apart from man, which is the only animal to have unique 'fingerprints'?
- **(a)** Baboon
- **(b)** Gorilla
- **(c)** Elephant
- **(d)** Koala Bear

6. What two words can be found on the bottom of a Ouija Board?
  (a) In Spirit
  (b) Absent Friends
  (c) Never Parted
  (d) Good Bye

7. Of what is a quire a unit of measurement?
  (a) Sound
  (b) Paper
  (c) Weight
  (d) Silver

8. Lightweight, half-lightweight and extra-lightweight are classes at which Olympic Sport?
  (a) Boxing
  (b) Judo
  (c) Wrestling
  (d) Weightlifting

9. Where, in the human body are the tarsals and metatarsals?
  (a) Hand
  (b) Leg
  (c) Foot
  (d) Back

10. From what is the Japanese drink Saki made?
  (a) Birds' nests
  (b) Egg
  (c) Rice
  (d) Honey

EVENTS OF THE 20TH CENTURY

All in chronological order

Example: The B of B = The Battle of Britain

The S F E

The S of the T

A E publishes the T of R

The R R

G S in G B

C L flies from NY to P

S V D M

B F on the NY S E

A J flies S from L to A

A H becomes C of G

The J B P H

A of M G

H and T C M E

Y G becomes F M in S

The G T R

J F K A in D

N A W on the M

D in the UK

B joins the C M

R N R as P of the U S

M T becomes the F B W P M

A K pronounces S of D on S R

QUIZ OF THE 20TH CENTURY

1. Events

(a) After 40 years of dictatorship, which country became a democracy on 27 December 1978?

(b) In October 1903, who in Britain founded the Women's Social and Political Union?

2. In what year?

(a) In what year did India gain independence, Princess Elizabeth marry Philip Mountbatten, and Charles Younger make the first supersonic air flight in California?

(b) In what year was Pope John Paul II shot and wounded in St Peter's Square in Rome, the Social Democrat Party formed by the Gang of Four in Britain, and Ronald Reagan sworn in as the 40th President of the USA?

3. A touch of nostalgia

(a) How is the female politician who was appointed US Ambassador to Ghana in 1974 better remembered?

(b) Can you name the US painter (1860–1961) who was born in Greenwich, New York? She only turned seriously to painting at the age of 67, specializing in naive and nostalgic scenes of farm life.

4. Men of the 20th century

(a) Name the king of Egypt who reigned from 1936 but was deposed by the military revolution of 1952 led by General Nasser. He died in exile in 1965.

(b) Who was the automobile engineer (1905–1988) who designed the Morris Minor in 1948 and the Mini in 1959?

5. Transport and Exploration

(a) Who, on 20 February 1962, became the first American to orbit the earth in space?

(b) Who was the Norwegian explorer who reached the South Pole on 15 December 1911?

6. Sport

(a) Who was the American boxer who became the first black fighter to win the World Heavyweight Championship, holding the title from 1908–1915?

(b) Which Australian tennis player was Wimbledon Lady Singles Champion in 1971 and 1980?

7. The Roaring Twenties

(a) In America, why was 28 October 1929 known as 'Black Friday'?

(b) Who, on 8 November 1923, attempted a coup d'état in Munich to overthrow the Bavarian government? He failed and served a term of imprisonment.

8. Disasters

(a) What was the name of the supertanker which ran aground in the Gulf of Alaska on 24 March 1989, spilling over 150,000 barrels of oil?

(b) An earthquake which on 3 February 1931 almost destroyed the cities of Napier and Hastings, occured in which country?

9. The Classics

(a) Who was the Irish playwright who won the Nobel Prize for literature in 1925?

(b) Who was the British composer who wrote 'A London Symphony' (1914), 'A Pastoral Symphony' (1921) and 'Hugh the Drover' (1924)?

10. Women of the 20th century

(a) Can you name the British nurse, who, in 1915 during World War I, was shot by the Germans for helping Allied soldiers to escape from occupied Brussels?

(b) Who was the Norwegian-born American

ice-skater and Hollywood film star who won 10 successive world titles from 1927 to 1936 and 3 Olympic gold medals (1928, 1932, and 1936) and whose films include *Sun Valley Serenade* (1941)?

11. Science
(a) What apparatus, used in underwater exploration, was invented in 1942 by Jacques Cousteau and Emile Gagnan?
(b) Can you name the South African surgeon who performed the first heart transplant operation in 1967?

12. The Movies
(a) Name the film for which Henry Fonda and Katharine Hepburn won Academy awards for Best Actor and Actress respectively in 1981.
(b) Who was the British debonair actor (1909–83) whose films include *Wuthering Heights* (1939), *Raffles* (1940), *Around the World in Eighty Days* (1956) and *Separate Tables* (1958)?

13. Wars
(a) What collective name is given to the two wars from 1912 to 1913, the first of which came when Montenegro, Bulgaria, Greece and Serbia joined together to fight Turkey and the second when Serbia, Greece, Romania and Turkey united against Bulgaria?
(b) The Six-Day War of 1967 came when Israel invaded which two countries?

14. Who Said?
(a) Who said 'This is not the end. It is not even the beginning of the end. But it is, perhaps, the end of the beginning'?
(b) Who said 'I guess it was because we were so completely unlike in every way, but, like bacon and eggs, we seemed to be about perfect together – but not so good apart'?

15. The World of Entertainment
(a) Who was the American vaudeville star known as the 'Last of the Red Hot Mamas', whose signature song was 'Some of These Days'?
(b) Who was the wide-eyed American comedian and song and dance man who appeared in Broadway musicals and films including *Kid Boots* (1932) and *Roman Scandals* (1933)?

16. Politics
(a) Who was known as 'The Lion of Judah'?
(b) What post was held by the Austrian diplomat Kurt Waldheim from 1972–81?

17. Popular Music
(a) Who was the American jazz musician whose compositions include 'Mood Indigo' and 'Don't Get Around Much Anymore'?
(b) Whose first commercial recording for Columbia was 'I've Got the Girl', which was recorded on 18 October 1926?

18. 20th-Century Icons
(a) Who was the youngest man ever to win a Nobel Peace Prize?
(b) For his starring role in the film of which of Shakespeare's plays did Laurence Olivier win the Academy award for Best Actor in 1948?

19. The Swinging Sixties
(a) Who was the author of the book *A Clockwork Orange* published in 1962?
(b) On 27 April 1964 the new state of Tanzania came into being after the merging of which two former countries?

20. Miscellaneous
(a) Which British newspaper was founded by Alfred Harmsworth on 2 November 1904?
(b) On 8 May 1980 the World Health Organisation formally declared the eradication of which disease?

1. Fruit bearing tree native to China
   A – – – – – –

2. Pen name of cookery writer Isabella Mary Mayson (1836–65)
   B – – – – –

3. The first Christian emperor of Rome
   C – – – – – – – – –

4. The male of the honey-bee
   D – – – –

5. Inventor of the Kodak camera
   E – – – – – –

6. Cape which is the most westerly point of the Spanish mainland
   F – – – – – – – –

7. Astronomer who was nearly burned at the stake for maintaining that the earth revolved around the sun
   G – – – – – –

8. Anglo-Saxon thane, nickname the Wake, who led the last English resistance against the Norman invaders
   H – – – – – – –

9. The first country to use an adhesive postage stamp
   I – – –

10. Mountain peak in Bernese Alps
    J – – – – – –

11. H. G. Wells novel on which the musical *Half a Sixpence* is based
    K – – – –

12. The national museum of art in Paris
    L – – – – –

13. Eponymous 19th century Texas ranger who refused to brand his calves
    M – – – – – – –

14. The Greek goddess of retribution
    N – – – – – –

15. The second largest city in Portugal
    O – – – – –

16. Plump bird of the pheasant family
    P – – – – – – – –

17. Fashion designer of the 'Swinging Sixties'
    Q – – – –

18. French statesman (1585–1642) known as the Red Eminence
    R – – – – – – – –

19. Biblical granddaughter of Herod the Great
    S – – – – –

20. Dr Who's flying police box
    T – – – – –

21. Fictional republic invented by Sir Thomas More
    U – – – – –

22. Religious cult popular in Haiti
    V – – – – –

23. 1969 New York state rock festival
    W – – – – – – – –

24. Persian king defeated by the Greeks
    X – – – – –

25. River of North America that rises in the Rocky Mountains and flows into the Bering Sea
    Y – – – –

26. Country formerly known as Southern Rhodesia
    Z – – – – – – –

SPIES OR LIES

In the world of espionage 'cover' means an alias, and 'music box' means transmitter. So are the other definitions true or false? Tick which is the correct box, either true or false.

	True	False
1. 'Spook' is slang for spy.	☐	☐
2. A 'bagman' specialises in stealing briefcases containing vital documents.	☐	☐
3. A 'shoe' is a false passport.	☐	☐
4. A 'wet job' is an operation on board a ship.	☐	☐
5. 'Illness' is Soviet slang for arrest.	☐	☐
6. 'Tapping' is intercepting telephone calls.	☐	☐
7. A 'flaps and seals man' is a spy working under cover as an itinerant circus performer.	☐	☐
8. A 'cobbler' is a spy who inserts radio transmitters into shoe heels.	☐	☐
9. 'Naked' is operating without cover.	☐	☐
10. 'Terminated with extreme prejudice' means mission aborted.	☐	☐

GIRL TALK

Below are ten quotations, each uttered by one of these famous women. Can you match who said what correctly?

INDIRA GANDHI

JUDY GARLAND

AGATHA CHRISTIE

MARY, QUEEN OF SCOTS

MARILYN MONROE

MADONNA

JANE AUSTEN

QUEEN VICTORIA

BARBARA BUSH

MAE WEST

1. I'm tough, ambitious and I know exactly what I want.

2. Never do anything yourself that others can do for you.

3. I married the first man I ever kissed. When I tell that to my children they just about throw up.

4. Say what you want about long dresses, but they cover a multitude of shins.

5. You cannot shake hands with a clenched fist.

6. I do not want people to be agreeable, as it saves me the trouble of liking them.

7. No more tears now, I will think about revenge.

8. I feel sure that no girl would go to the altar if she knew all.

9. I was born at the age of twelve on an MGM lot.

10. I've been on a calendar, but never on time.

THE WEIRD AND WONDERFUL TRIVIA QUIZ

1. What was first created by Capt. Hanson Gregory Crockett?
   - **(a)** The potato chip
   - **(b)** Holes in doughnuts
   - **(c)** Chicken-à-la-king
   - **(d)** The Capitol Cab Co of New York

2. 'Honorificabilitudinitatibus' is the longest word in the works of which writer?
   - **(a)** Mark Twain
   - **(b)** Lewis Carroll
   - **(c)** Charles Dickens
   - **(d)** William Shakespeare

3. What is Arachibutyrophobia the fear of?
   - **(a)** Going to sleep in case a spider crawls under the bedclothes
   - **(b)** Eating a peanut butter sandwich in case the gooey peanut butter sticks to the roof of the mouth
   - **(c)** Dreaming of spiders
   - **(d)** Putting buttered bread on the dining table in case any insect, but particularly a spider crawls over it

4. In 1882 a weird and wonderful new type of alarm was invented. How did it work?
   - **(a)** It sprayed the sleeper with a fine jet of water
   - **(b)** It tipped 20 wooden blocks onto the sleeper
   - **(c)** It stuck a fine needle into a sleeping dog so that the resultant commotion woke the sleeper
   - **(d)** The bed tilted sideways and slid the sleeper gently out of bed

5. What did Max Baer say to Primo Carnera when they both fell to the canvas in the first round of their World Heavyweight Championship fight in June 1934?

   - **(a)** Stay there, I'll help you up
   - **(b)** Let's call it a draw
   - **(c)** It's hardly worth your while getting up
   - **(d)** Last one up's a sissy

6. For what purpose did Dr John Pemberton brew the first batch of Coca-Cola in 1886?
   - **(a)** As a sexual stimulant
   - **(b)** As a laxative
   - **(c)** As a cure for a hangover, stomachache and headache
   - **(d)** As an alternative to smoking

7. What was unusual about the 29 stagecoach robberies carried out by Californian Charles E. Bolton, otherwise known as Black Bart?
   - **(a)** He only stole men's watches
   - **(b)** He only stole the horses driving the stagecoach
   - **(c)** His guns were never loaded
   - **(d)** He made all his victims strip naked and then stole their clothes

8. Apart from writing numerous musical compositions including 200 cantatas and the Brandenburg Concertos, how many children did Johann Sebastian Bach find time to father?
   - **(a)** 5   **(b)** 10   **(c)** 15   **(d)** 20

9. Whose professional boxing-ring name was Marty O'Brien in his youth?
   - **(a)** Bob Hope
   - **(b)** Bill Clinton
   - **(c)** Frank Sinatra
   - **(d)** Ronald Reagan

10. What is klazomania?
    - **(a)** Excessive impulse to write
    - **(b)** Compulsive shouting
    - **(c)** A morbid impulse to pull out one's hair
    - **(d)** A desire to eat cornflakes continually

Some sayings are familiar to everyone, but others are not so well-known. Here are a number of fairly obscure ones. From the choices given can you work out the correct meaning?

1. Kiss the gunner's daughter
   (a) To be lashed to a gun and flogged
   (b) Be forced into a shotgun marriage
   (c) Marry below your station

2. Born in the purple
   (a) Receive an inheritance
   (b) Be a gypsy
   (c) High and wealthy

3. Up to putty
   (a) A good job, well done
   (b) No good, valueless, of bad quality
   (c) To have almost finished the job

4. Cloud castle
   (a) A successful venture
   (b) A dismal failure
   (c) A visionary scheme

5. To blow a coal
   (a) To explode angrily
   (b) To stir up strife
   (c) To be at a state of exhaustion

6. The devil's playthings
   (a) Playing cards
   (b) Matches
   (c) Fireworks

7. Drug in the market
   (a) So common as to be unsaleable
   (b) Anything which destroys stability
   (c) A rare commodity

8. To face down
   (a) To fall asleep
   (b) To start afresh
   (c) To confront defiantly

9. To feed the fishes
   (a) To make a little go a long way
   (b) To be drowned
   (c) To go on a fishing expedition

10. To stand in the gap
    (a) To take up one of several fielding positions in cricket
    (b) To come to someone's financial rescue
    (c) To expose oneself for the protection of others

1. How tall was King Charles I of England before he was beheaded?
   (a) 4 feet 9 inches
   (b) 5 feet 1 inch
   (c) 5 feet 3 inches
   (d) 5 feet 5 inches

2. Prospero, Miranda, Ferdinand, Ariel and Caliban are characters in which Shakespeare play?
   (a) *The Tempest*
   (b) *Twelfth Night*
   (c) *Love's Labour's Lost*
   (d) *The Winter's Tale*

3. The distance over which a full marathon is run is 26 miles and how many yards?
   (a) 325
   (b) 345
   (c) 385
   (d) 415

4. What have you got if you are suffering from singultus?
   (a) A hangover
   (b) Hiccups
   (c) Tennis elbow
   (d) A sore throat

5. The Kariba Dam stands on which river?
   (a) Nile
   (b) Zambezi
   (c) Congo
   (d) Zaire

6. What, in Russia, would be contained in a Samovar?
   (a) Vodka
   (b) Coins
   (c) Tea
   (d) Ashes

7. How many periods are there in an ice-hockey game?
   (a) 2
   (b) 3
   (c) 4
   (d) 5

8. What is bruxomania?
   (a) Compulsive shouting
   (b) Excessive impulse to write
   (c) Compulsive and continual crunching of the teeth together with intermittent grinding
   (d) A morbid impulse to pull out one's own hair

9. Who is Gautama Siddhartha, born in India in 500 BC better known as?
   (a) Mohammed
   (b) Buddah
   (c) Abu Bekr
   (d) Ataturk

10. What is an Eskimo's mukluk a type of?
    (a) Hat
    (b) Boat
    (c) Igloo
    (d) Knife

SPORTING ANAGRAM QUIZ

All the following are past and present sporting giants of the 20th century

1. Golfer: GOT ROWDIES

2. Racing driver: TWICE TAKE JARS

3. Footballer: ARSENAL HARE

4. Rider: INCLUDE RANGE

5. Tennis player: INVARIANT LARVA ATOM

6. Jockey: GO GET TRIPLETS

7. Tennis player: REPEAT SPASM

8. Footballer: BAN TORCH LOBBY

9. Athlete: THE MOODY PLANS

10. Skater: LIVELY TROJAN

11. Cricketer: SAW NEAR HEN

12. Athlete: FIRM BATH AWAITED

13. Tennis player: RAISE SAD NAG

14. Rugby player: BEND ARROW

15. Boxer: OR WICKED BID

16. Snooker player: TENDER HYPHENS

17. Footballer: GO GET BEERS

18. Tennis player: OCEAN SMILES

19. Cricketer: VAPID ELK

20. Golfer: LEERING COMMOTION

PHOBIAS

Zoophobia is a fear of animals and claustrophobia a fear of confined spaces. Can you match column A – the name of the phobia, with column B – what it is the fear of?

A	B
Anthrophobia	Standing
Potophobia	Poverty
Ailourophobia	Ice
Hypegiaphobia	Gravity
Kleptophobia	Blushing
Oikophobia	People
Barophobia	Work
Rypophobia	Mice
Stasiphobia	Ruin
Ereuthophobia	Drinks
Chronophobia	Sailing
Cynophobia	Cats
Peniaphobia	Light
Ergophobia	Dogs
Toxiphobia	Home
Kristallophobia	Responsiblity
Ommatophobia	Poisoning
Atephobia	Stealing
Photophobia	Time
Musophobia	Eyes

FAMOUS NAMES

From the clues given below, pair up two sets
of three letters from the grid to form
20 famous names.

OCK	NER	GAN	HUG	NCE	CHO	GAL	MUG
ATA	HUB	SON	TER	HES	ZAP	ARN	OUK
ROE	PIN	FAR	THA	KEL	WAG	MON	KRU
LES	TON	ERH	OLD	ALC	MOR	WOL	SPE
BLE	SEY	ABE	GER	WIL	POR	ARD	VIN

1. Welsh buccaneer
2. Polish composer
3. Scottish architect
4. American general
5. British physicist
6. American composer
7. German composer
8. English churchman
9. Mexican revolutionary
10. English scientist
11. English aviator
12. Zimbabwean statesman
13. American president
14. South African statesman
15. Greek philosopher
16. West German statesman
17. American film actress
18. Egyptian king
19. American astronomer
20. English poet

PORTMANTEAU WORDS

A portmanteau word is one formed by combining
together parts of other words. For example, the
word MOTEL is derived from the two words
MOTOR and HOTEL. Can you say what
portmanteau words are derived from each
set of two words below?

1. FLAME / GLARE
2. BREAKFAST / LUNCH
3. SNACK / MASH
4. SQUIRM / WIGGLE
5. GLAMOUR / RITZ
6. FLOUNCE / FOUNDER
7. CHUCKLE / SNORT
8. SMOKE / FOG
9. FANTASTIC / FABULOUS
10. GLEAM / SHIMMER

1. Which name, in Norse, means ruler of all?
   - (a) Eric
   - (b) Harold
   - (c) Carl
   - (d) Stephen

2. Which one of these animals can travel the fastest?
   - (a) Coyote
   - (b) Greyhound
   - (c) Whippet
   - (d) Jackal

3. Which of the Seven Wonders of the World was at Ephesus?
   - (a) The Tomb of Mausolus
   - (b) The Statue of Zeus
   - (c) The Temple of Artemis
   - (d) The Hanging Gardens

4. In 1970 Mission Control received the message, 'Houston, we've got a problem here', from which spacecraft?
   - (a) Apollo 13
   - (b) Apollo X
   - (c) Apollo 15
   - (d) Apollo V

5. Which country's flag consists of six horizontal red and white stripes, and a white star on a dark blue background in the top left-hand corner?
   - (a) Indonesia
   - (b) Liberia
   - (c) Cuba
   - (d) Chile

6. What are double loops, radial loops, arches, whorls and ulna loops?
   - (a) Movements in aerobics
   - (b) Types of stitches
   - (c) Movements in freeskating
   - (d) Fingerprints

7. In the Old Testament, who was the husband of Zipporah?
   - (a) Jonah
   - (b) Moses
   - (c) Jethro
   - (d) Noah

8. What type of furniture are Davenports and Escritoires?
   - (a) Wooden chairs
   - (b) Low cabinets
   - (c) Writing desks
   - (d) Tables

9. In what is an oenologist an expert?
   - (a) Wine
   - (b) Ghosts
   - (c) Whales and dolphins
   - (d) Music

10. Which island group was formerly called 'The Friendly Isles'?
    - (a) Falklands
    - (b) Tonga
    - (c) Solomon
    - (d) Windward

1. Youngest daughter of Russian Czar Nicholas II

    A – – – – – – – –

2. Classic composition of Maurice Ravel

    B – – – – –

3. Australian parrot with distinctive crest of head feathers

    C – – – – – – –

4. 1971 movie starring Dennis Weaver in a car being terrorised and chased by a tank truck

    D – – –

5. The study of work

    E – – – – – – – –

6. Pre-decimal British coin

    F – – – – –

7. First left-handed US President

    G – – – – – – –

8. Former Pinkerton detective who wrote the novels *The Maltese Falcon* and *The Thin Man*

    H – – – – – –

9. What was described by Mark Twain as 'mother of history, grandmother of legend and grandmother of tradition'?

    I – – – –

10. The SI unit of energy

    J – – – –

11. Swiss alpine winter skiing resort

    K – – – – – –

12. Term applied to the 14th-century followers of the English theologian John Wycliffe

    L – – – – – –

13. First breed of horse used by American Indians

    M – – – – – –

14. 14th century French astrologer

    N – – – – – – – – –

15. American sharpshooter born Phoebe Annie Moses

    O – – – – –

16. In Greek mythology, the god of wealth

    P – – – –

17. A fundamental component of matter; symbol q

    Q – – – –

18. American mountain which contains the carved heads of four American Presidents

    R – – – – – –

19. Character played by Ray Bolger in the 1939 movie *The Wizard of Oz*

S – – – – – – –

20. The largest lake in South America

T – – – – – –

21. General name for a mammal whose toes end in hooves rather than claws

U – – – – – –

22. Mr Spock's home planet in *Star Trek*

V – – – – –

23. The capital of Namibia

W – – – – – –

24. The most widely used method of photocopying

X – – – – – – – –

25. Residential suburb on the northern edge of Greater New York

Y – – – – – –

26. The inventor of Esperanto

Z – – – – – – –

CHOOSE A NUMBER

3 4 6 7
8 9 12 13
20 24 45 46
66 102 116 206

Match each of the sixteen numbers in the array above with one of the sixteen statements below:

(a) Standard Zones of International Time

(b) Kings of England named Henry

(c) Colours in a Rainbow

(d) Chromosomes in a Human Cell

(e) Days of Creation

(f) Degrees in an Octant

(g) Movements in a Symphony

(h) Caesars of Ancient Rome

(i) Bones in the Human Ear

(j) Innings in a Baseball Game

(k) Bones in the Human Body

(l) Years slept by Rip Van Winkle

(m) Floors in the Empire State Building

(n) Stripes on the American Flag

(o) Books in the King James Bible

(p) Years in the Hundred Years War

1. The swimming star of the 1932 Olympics was Buster Crabbe. What character did he go on to play in the movies?
   - **(a)** Tarzan
   - **(b)** The Lone Ranger
   - **(c)** Flash Gordon
   - **(d)** Superman

2. Which actor was described by the *New York Times* as 'both a human tempest and an actor of sizeable gifts'?
   - **(a)** Sean Penn
   - **(b)** Kenneth Brannagh
   - **(c)** Marlon Brando
   - **(d)** Dennis Hopper

3. Who plays Albert Einstein in the 1994 movie *IQ*?
   - **(a)** Walter Matthau
   - **(b)** Tim Curry
   - **(c)** Burgess Meredith
   - **(d)** Frank Langella

4. In which 1945 Hitchcock classic does Ingrid Bergman play a psychiatrist trying to uncover Gregory Peck's hang-ups?
   - **(a)** *Spellbound*
   - **(b)** *Saboteur*
   - **(c)** *Suspicion*
   - **(d)** *Notorious*

5. At the very start of his career Mickey Mouse was briefly not known as Mickey, but by which other name?
   - **(a)** Maurice
   - **(b)** Montague
   - **(c)** Mortimer
   - **(d)** Maxwell

6. Who, in the 1992 movie, was 'The Lawnmower Man'?
   - **(a)** Pierce Brosnan
   - **(b)** Liam Neeson
   - **(c)** Jeff Fahey
   - **(d)** Lukas Haas

7. The team of Robert Redford and Paul Newman (*Butch Cassidy and the Sundance Kid*, 1969) were reunited for which 1973 movie?
   - **(a)** *The Towering Inferno*
   - **(b)** *The Great Gatsby*
   - **(c)** *The Sting*
   - **(d)** *The Mackintosh Man*

8. In the Beatles film *Yellow Submarine*, who are the villains?
   - **(a)** The Pepperpots
   - **(b)** The Red Face Mob
   - **(c)** The Squeegees
   - **(d)** The Meanies

9. In which film does Bette Davis speak the classic line 'Jerry, don't let's ask for the moon, we have the stars'?
   - **(a)** *Now Voyager*
   - **(b)** *Of Human Bondage*
   - **(c)** *Jezebel*
   - **(d)** *All This, And Heaven Too*

10. Who plays the nurse who tends Ralph Fiennes in *The English Patient*?
   - **(a)** Juliette Binoche
   - **(b)** Gina Gershon
   - **(c)** Renee Zellweger
   - **(d)** Illeana Douglas

11. Who shot Liberty Valance?
    (a) James Stewart
    (b) John Wayne
    (c) Lee Marvin
    (d) Gene Pitney

12. In which movie did Humphrey Bogart play Capt. Philip Francis Queeg?
    (a) *China Clipper*
    (b) *The African Queen*
    (c) *Action in the North Atlantic*
    (d) *The Caine Mutiny*

13. Who played Demi Moore's husband in *Indecent Proposal*?
    (a) Robert Redford
    (b) Hugh Grant
    (c) Woody Harrelson
    (d) Bruce Willis

14. Recruited from 300 hopeful candidates, what was the original name of the dog which in 1943 became known as Lassie?
    (a) Chum
    (b) Bongo
    (c) Pal
    (d) Bonnie

15. What did Ingrid Bergman really say in *Casablanca*?
(a) 'Play it again Sam . . . play "As Time Goes By"'
(b) 'Play it Sam . . . play "As Time Goes By"'
(c) 'Play "As Time Goes By" . . . just for me, Sam'
(d) 'Play it for me Sam . . . play "As Time Goes By"'

16. Which 6-year-old actress played Mia Farrow and Bruce Dern's daughter in the 1974 movie *The Great Gatsby*?
    (a) Mariel Hemingway
    (b) Jennifer Beals
    (c) Sean Young
    (d) Patsy Kensit

17. Of the Marx Brothers, whose real name was Adolph?
    (a) Chico
    (b) Gummo
    (c) Groucho
    (d) Harpo

18. In the 1992 movie, *A League of their Own*, Tom Hanks is the manager of a team of women – in what sport?
    (a) Tennis
    (b) Basketball
    (c) Football
    (d) Baseball

19. In the 1958 movie *Cat on a Hot Tin Roof*, what is Elizabeth Taylor's response to Paul Newman's question, 'What is the victory of a cat on a hot tin roof?'?
    (a) 'I guess I don't know, is it really a victory?'
    (b) 'It's her choice to be there'
    (c) 'Just staying on it, I guess. Long as she wants'
    (d) 'She can jump off, anytime she wants'

20. In which 1949 film did Katharine Hepburn and Spencer Tracey play married attorneys who were opposing council in a court case?
    (a) *Pat and Mike*
    (b) *Woman of the Year*
    (c) *State of the Union*
    (d) *Adam's Rib*

WEDDING ANNIVERSARY QUIZ

Match the gift with the correct year

YEAR	GIFT
FIRST	LACE
SECOND	CRYSTAL
THIRD	COTTON
FIFTH	STEEL
SEVENTH	WOOD
TENTH	PAPER
ELEVENTH	IVORY
THIRTEENTH	TIN
FOURTEENTH	LEATHER
FIFTEENTH	WOOL

LITERARY THEME QUIZ

These are the first lines from 10 classic literary works. Can you name in each case the title of the work and the author?

1. 'Alice was beginning to get very tired of sitting by her sister on the bank ...'

2. 'It was the best of times, it was the worst of times ...'

3. 'Most of the adventures recorded in this book really occurred; one or two were experiences of my own, the rest of those boys who were schoolmates of mine ...'

4. 'Mrs Rachel Lynde lived just where the Avonlea main road dipped down into a little hollow ...'

5. 'I have just returned from a visit to my landlord – the solitary neighbour that I shall be troubled with ...'

6. Antonio: 'In sooth, I know not why I am so sad. . . .'

7. 'Once upon a midnight dreary, while I pondered, weak and weary, . . .'

8. 'You will rejoice to hear that no disaster has accompanied the commencement of an enterprise which you have regarded with such evil forebodings ...'

9. 'Mr Phileas Fogg lived, in 1872, at No.7, Saville Row, Burlington Gardens ...'

10. 'The hare was once boasting of his speed before the other animals ...'

Answers are entered starting at the appropriate number and spiralling towards the centre. Word lengths are indicated, and each answer begins with one or more letters from the end of the previous word.

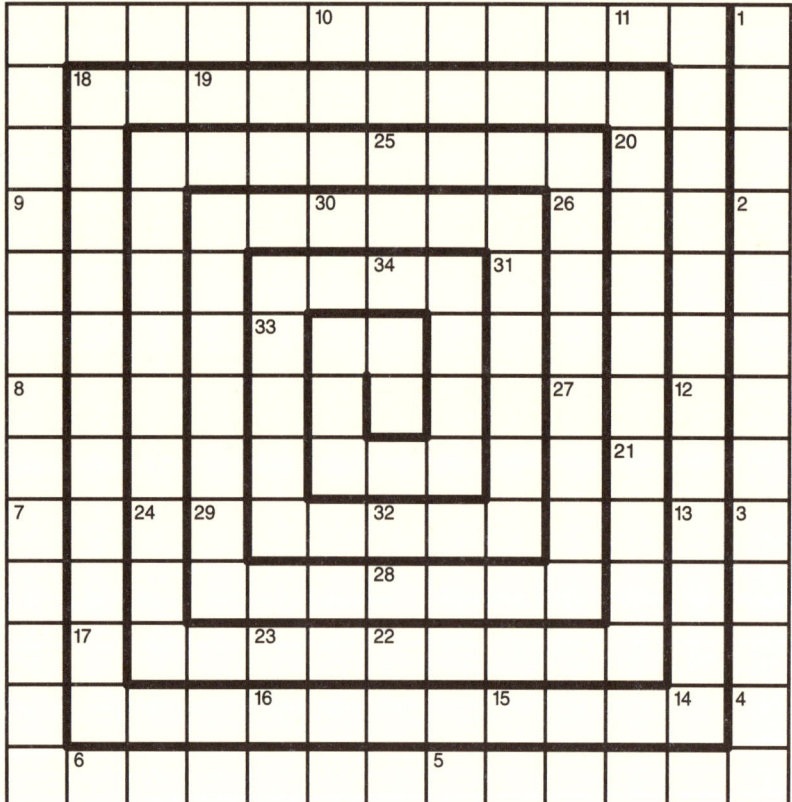

17. Type of cultivated cabbage (11)
18. The Northern stoat (6)
19. The study of minerals (10)
20. An instrument consisting of a rapidly spinning wheel (9)
21. The founder of modern astronomy (1473–1543) (10)
22. US soldier killed at the Little Big Horn (6)
23. The currency of Britain (8)
24. The scientific study of language (11)
25. The lowest layer of clouds in the atmosphere (7)
26. The simplest of the five main orders of classical architecture (6)
27. Christian festival celebrated 2 February (9)
28. Poet Laureate 1930–67 (9)
29. Thrush, found in Greenland since 1937 (9)
30. American patriot who rode from Charleston to Lexington (6)
31. The capital of Iceland (9)
32. Project that was the first successful landing mission to Mars (6)
33. Swedish film actress who preferred seclusion (5)
34. Surname of Henry IV of England (11)

CLUES

1. America's Sunflower State (6)
2. Siegfried, British poet and novelist (7)
3. The Asiatic wild ass (6)
4. The cranesbill or pelargonium (8)
5. Bird with inflatable air sac (8)
6. The most famous of King Arthur's knights (8)
7. Sacred plant of Egypt (5)
8. French modeller in wax (7)
9. Middle east kingdom (5,6)

10. A combined test of cross-country skiing and rifle shooting (8)
11. Author of 'The Song of Hiawatha' (10)
12. Manchester-born painter of industrial landscapes (5)
13. Short-billed variety of woodpecker (7)
14. French statesman and financier (1732–1804) (6)
15. Paraffin (8)
16. Roman writer and author of a history of Rome (6)

ACROSS

1. Another name for water (5,3)

7. In Norse mythology the god who gave one eye to the Giant Mimir in exchange for wisdom (4)

8. The first major engagement of the English Civil War (8)

9. Sir Samuel — (1824–1901) who had a military officer's belt named after him (6)

10. Province in the Irish Republic (6)

11. An ancient game for two players using counters (3)

12. 1942 Walt Disney classic movie (5)

14. Greek beauty whose abduction caused the Trojan War (5)

16. The SI unit of electrical resistance (3)

18. Turkish mountain said to be the landing place of Noah's Ark (6)

20. British Prime Minister 1945–51 (6)

22. A motorway in Germany (8)

23. A soft white French cheese (4)

24. Royal castle and estate in Grampion, Scotland (8)

DOWN

1. Small semi-independent state between France and Spain (7)

2. US Vice-President under Richard Nixon (5)

3. Kingdom of Northern Europe (6)

4. — vitae, evergreen tree and source of durable timber (6)

5. Capital of Nord department, France, near to Belgian frontier (5)

6. Lover of Pyramus in an ancient Babylonian story (6)

13. French film actress discovered by Roger Vadim (6)

15. Prophet of the Old Testament (7)

16. The capital of Canada (6)

17. A wine bottle containing the equivalent of two normal bottles (6)

19. The place where Joan of Arc was burned at the stake (5)

21. The second longest river in Italy (5)

Numbers Game
page 55

3 Legs on a Tripod
4 Suits in a Deck of Cards
7 Dwarfs in Snow White
8 Legs on a Spider
9 Symphonies by Beethoven
10 Little Indian Boys
10 Provinces in Canada
11 Fathoms in a Chain
11 Players in a Cricket Team
12 Apostles at the Last Supper
14 Days in a Fortnight
20 Years slept by Rip Van Winkle
25 Years of Marriage for a Silver Anniversary
30 Days Hath September
32 Degrees Fahrenheit at which Water Freezes
64 Squares on a Chessboard
500 Sheets in a Ream
1000 Ships Launched by the Face of Helen of Troy
1440 Minutes in a Day
5280 Feet in a Mile

Trivia Miscellany pages 55–6

1. (b)
2. (d)
3. (a)
4. (d)
5. (d)
6. (d)
7. (b)
8. (b)
9. (c)
10. (c)

Events of the 20th Century
page 56

The San Francisco Earthquake
The sinking of the *Titanic*
Albert Einstein publishes the *Theory of Relativity*
The Russian Revolution
General Strike in Great Britain
Charles Lindbergh flies from New York to Paris
St Valentine's Day Massacre
Black Friday on the New York Stock Exchange
Amy Johnson flies solo from London to Australia
Adolf Hitler becomes Chancellor of Germany
The Japanese bomb Pearl Harbor
Assassination of Mahatma Gandhi
Hillary and Tensing climb Mount Everest
Yuri Gagarin becomes first man in space
The Great Train Robbery
John F Kennedy assassinated in Dallas
Neil Armstrong walks on the moon
Decimalisation in the United Kingdom
Britain joins the Common Market
Richard Nixon resigns as President of the United States
Margaret Thatcher becomes the first British woman Prime Minister
Ayatollah Khomeini pronounces sentence of death on Salman Rushdie

Quiz of the 20th Century
pages 57–8

1. (a) Spain
   (b) Mrs Emmeline Pankhurst
2. (a) 1947
   (b) 1981
3. (a) as child movie star, Shirley Temple
   (b) Grandma Moses

4. (a) Farouk
   (b) Sir Alec Arnold Constantine Issigonis
5. (a) Lieut-Col John Glenn
   (b) Roald Amundsen
6. (a) Jack Johnson
   (b) Evonne Goolagong
7. (a) It was the collapse of the US Stock Exchange in New York and the beginning of The Great Depression
   (b) Adolf Hitler
8. (a) Exxon Valdez
   (b) New Zealand
9. (a) George Bernard Shaw
   (b) Ralph Vaughan Williams
10. (a) Edith Cavell
    (b) Sonja Henie
11. (a) The aqualung
    (b) Dr Christiaan Barnard
12. (a) *On Golden Pond*
    (b) David Niven
13. (a) The Balkan Wars
    (b) Egypt and Jordan
14. (a) Sir Winston Churchill (in a speech at the Mansion House)
    (b) Oliver Hardy (when explaining why he thought people found the Laurel and Hardy partnership so funny)
15. (a) Sophie Tucker
    (b) Eddie Cantor
16. (a) Haile Selassie
    (b) Secretary General of the United Nations
17. (a) Duke Ellington
    (b) Bing Crosby
18. (a) Martin Luther King Jr
    (b) Hamlet
19. (a) Anthony Burgess
    (b) Tanganyika and Zanzibar
20. (a) The *Daily Mirror*
    (b) Smallpox

A-Z of Trivia 1 *page 59*

1. Apricot
2. Beeton
3. Constantine
4. Drone
5. Eastman
6. Finisterre
7. Galileo
8. Hereward
9. Iraq
10. Jungfrau
11. Kipps
12. Louvre
13. Maverick
14. Nemesis
15. Oporto
16. Partridge
17. Quant
18. Richelieu
19. Salome
20. Tardis
21. Utopia
22. Voodoo
23. Woodstock
24. Xerxes
25. Yukon
26. Zimbabwe

Spies or Lies *page 60*

1. True
2. False; he is a secret agent who pays bribes
3. True
4. False; it is an operation where blood is shed
5. True
6. True
7. False; he is an expert in the undetected opening and closing of mail
8. False; he is a forger
9. True
10. False; it means murdered

Girl Talk page 60

1. Madonna
2. Agatha Christie
3. Barbara Bush
4. Mae West
5. Indira Gandhi
6. Jane Austen
7. Mary, Queen of Scots
8. Queen Victoria
9. Judy Garland
10. Marilyn Monroe

The Weird and Wonderful Trivia Quiz page 61

1. (b)
2. (d)
3. (b)
4. (b)
5. (d)
6. (c)
7. (c)
8. (d)
9. (c)
10. (b)

Triple Choice page 62

1. (a)
2. (c)
3. (b) (Australian slang)
4. (c)
5. (b)
6. (a)
7. (a)
8. (c)
9. (b)
10. (c)

More Trivia page 63

1. (a)
2. (a)
3. (c)
4. (b)
5. (b)
6. (c)
7. (b)
8. (c)
9. (b)
10. (b)

Sporting Anagram Quiz page 64

1. Tiger Woods
2. Jackie Stewart
3. Alan Shearer
4. Lucinda Green
5. Martina Navratilova
6. Lester Piggott
7. Pete Sampras
8. Bobby Charlton
9. Daley Thompson
10. Jayne Torvill
11. Shane Warne
12. Fatima Whitbread
13. Andre Agassi
14. Rob Andrew
15. Riddick Bowe
16. Stephen Hendry
17. George Best
18. Monica Seles
19. Kapil Dev
20. Colin Montgomerie

Phobias *page 64*

ANTHROPHOBIA: people
POTOPHOBIA: drinks
AILOUROPHOBIA: cats
HYPEGIAPHOBIA: responsibility
KLEPTOPHOBIA: stealing
OIKOPHOBIA: home
BAROPHOBIA: gravity
RYPOPHOBIA: sailing
STASIPHOBIA: standing
EREUTHOPHOBIA: blushing
CHRONOPHOBIA: time
CYNOPHOBIA: dogs
PENIAPHOBIA: poverty
ERGOPHOBIA: work
TOXIPHOBIA: poisoning
KRISTALLOPHOBIA: ice
OMMATOPHOBIA: eyes
ATEPHOBIA: ruin
PHOTOPHOBIA: light
MUSOPHOBIA: mice

Famous Names *page 65*

1. Morgan
2. Chopin
3. Spence
4. Arnold
5. Kelvin
6. Porter
7. Wagner
8. Wolsey
9. Zapata
10. Galton
11. Alcock
12. Mugabe
13. Wilson
14. Kruger
15. Thales
16. Erhard
17. Monroe
18. Farouk
19. Hubble
20. Hughes

Portmanteau Words *page 65*

1. FLARE
2. BRUNCH
3. SMASH
4. SQUIGGLE
5. GLITZ
6. FLOUNDER
7. CHORTLE
8. SMOG
9. FANTABULOUS
10. GLIMMER

Teaser Time *page 66*

1. (a)
2. (a)
3. (c)
4. (a)
5. (b)
6. (d)
7. (b)
8. (c)
9. (a)
10. (b)

A-Z of Trivia 2 *pages 67–8*

1. Anastasia
2. Bolero
3. Cockatoo
4. Duel
5. Ergonomics
6. Florin
7. Garfield
8. Hammett
9. India
10. Joule
11. Klosters
12. Lollards
13. Mustang
14. Nostradamus
15. Oakley
16. Pluto
17. Quark
18. Rushmore
19. Scarecrow
20. Titicaca
21. Ungulate
22. Vulcan
23. Windhoek
24. Xerography
25. Yonkers
26. Zamenhof

Choose a Number *page 68*

(a) 24
(b) 8
(c) 7
(d) 46
(e) 6
(f) 45
(g) 4
(h) 12
(i) 3
(j) 9
(k) 206
(l) 20
(m) 102
(n) 13
(o) 66
(p) 116

Movie Quiz *pages 69–70*

1. (c)
2. (a)
3. (a)
4. (a)
5. (c)
6. (c)
7. (c)
8. (d)
9. (a)
10. (a)
11. (b)
12. (d)
13. (c)
14. (c)
15. (b)
16. (d)
17. (d)
18. (d)
19. (c)
20. (d)

Wedding Anniversary Quiz
page 71

First – Cotton
Second – Paper
Third – Leather
Fifth – Wood
Seventh – Wool
Tenth – Tin
Eleventh – Steel
Thirteenth – Lace
Fourteenth – Ivory
Fifteenth – Crystal

Literary Theme Quiz page 71

1. *Alice's Adventures in Wonderland*
Lewis Carroll
2. *A Tale of Two Cities*
Charles Dickens
3. *The Adventures of Tom Sawyer*
Mark Twain
4. *Anne of Green Gables*
Lucy Maud Montgomery
5. *Wuthering Heights*
Emily Jane Brontë
6. *The Merchant of Venice*
William Shakespeare
7. *The Raven*
Edgar Allan Poe
8. *Frankenstein*
Mary Shelley
9. *Around the World in 80 Days*
Jules Verne
10. *The Hare and the Tortoise*
Aesop

Wraparound Crossword page 72

```
D I A R A B I A T H L O K
U E R M I N E R A L O N A
A W S T I C S T R A G G N
S O I F A R E V E T Y F S
S L U D A R B O R U R E A
U F G L G O K L E S O L S
T I N E N R E I Y C S L S
O L I I B G N K A C O O
L U F K I V A J N O W O
E A R E S A M E L D P R N
C C E T S U C I N R E Y A
N E N E S O R E K C E N G
A L L E R B M U I N A R E
```

Quiz Word page 73

```
A D A M S A L E       L
N   G   W   I     T   I
O D I N   E D G E H I L L
O   E   D   N   I L
B R O W N E   U L S T E R
R       N I M   B
B A M B I       H E L E N
    A   O H M       Z
A R A R A T   A T T L E E
O   D   T G   I   K
A U T O B A H N   B R I E
E   T   W U   E E
N   B A L M O R A L
```

JUST FOR KIDS

CROSSWORD ONE

CLUES

Across

3. Piece of land for public recreation (4)
6. Railway vehicle (5)
8. Biblical character of great physical strength (6)
9. Not sour (5)
13. Correct or true (5)
15. Become visible (6)
16. Light, moderate purple colour (5)
17. Sympathy felt for the sufferings of another person (4)

Down

1. Monarch's jewelled head-dress (5)
2. Sensible (4)
4. As well (4)
5. Monarch (4)
7. Not artificial (7)
10. In the front (5)
11. Draw breath in horror (4)
12. Dot (4)
14. Part of the eye (4)

NAME GAME

All these are anagrams of boys and girls' names.
See if you can find yourself or any of your friends
among them.
Example: SHINE TAPE = STEPHANIE

EGG ROE	BET GIRL
IN TRAM	CHERISH PORT
BASE SAINT	THE ANKLE
RIDING	HAMLET
A MAPLE	CALL MOM
SHIN COAL	RICH SAINT
AIRMAN	ORDINALS
AIR TAILS	REAL ONE
RAVELLING	LOUD GAS
ALIENS	A LINEN HAT
RAG HAM	HE CARL
TALE IAN	RAN ADS
LARGE DIN	OLD DAN
ILL GAIN	NO RASH
NICE SHIRT	FOGEY REF
COLD RIFF	IN EXAM
CLIP RAILS	ENABLE LAN

ROUTE 66

This is a journey on the famous Route 66 in the
USA. On its journey from East to West the
highway passes through eight states. Can you solve
the anagrams to discover the names of the states?

IS OIL NIL

MUIR IS SO

AN ASKS

HOOK ALMA

TAXES

ONCE WE MIX

NAZI OAR

FAIR NICOLA

COLOURS

Find the colours listed below in the grid by reading forwards, backwards, horizontally, vertically or diagonally, but always in a straight line.

U	B	V	L	C	H	D	A	M	A	S	K	E
L	R	M	A	R	O	O	N	T	T	A	N	V
T	O	B	V	E	R	S	U	R	A	P	I	I
R	W	E	E	A	F	N	A	K	Y	P	P	L
A	N	O	N	M	T	W	A	F	K	H	R	O
M	B	G	D	S	B	L	U	E	F	I	V	G
A	E	C	E	E	C	F	B	G	P	R	I	I
R	P	H	R	L	Y	A	U	U	A	E	O	D
I	C	R	E	N	E	E	R	G	N	B	L	N
N	Y	M	I	R	L	P	N	L	N	M	E	I
E	O	F	U	C	L	R	S	T	E	A	T	I
N	O	Z	U	E	O	N	X	N	I	T	Y	I
C	A	L	I	L	W	T	F	B	S	T	X	C

AMBER	CHESTNUT	LAVENDER	PINK	SIENNA
APRICOT	CREAM	LEMON	PURPLE	STRAWBERRY
AUBURN	CYAN	LILAC	RED	ULTRAMARINE
AZURE	DAMASK	MAROON	SAFFRON	VIOLET
BLUE	GREEN	OLIVE	SAPPHIRE	YELLOW
BROWN	INDIGO	ORANGE	SCARLET	

GAMES

Find the games listed below in the grid, reading forwards, backwards, horizontally, vertically or diagonally, but always in a straight line. One of the games in the list is not in the grid – which one?

T	N	K	W	H	I	S	T	B	O	W	L	S	E
G	C	O	L	O	P	A	X	R	E	K	O	P	D
A	R	C	H	E	R	Y	O	I	N	O	F	T	H
R	I	S	N	A	P	U	S	D	I	C	E	G	G
B	B	T	C	Q	L	E	E	G	G	U	N	O	B
G	B	C	W	E	C	C	L	E	Q	O	C	L	P
D	A	R	T	S	H	U	B	O	J	L	I	F	H
B	G	T	P	E	U	S	R	H	T	W	N	Z	Y
T	E	S	S	O	R	C	A	L	O	A	G	B	N
L	Z	S	E	A	N	M	M	U	I	D	I	K	G
J	O	S	H	I	N	T	Y	A	Q	N	U	F	Y
O	L	O	S	Z	I	A	O	F	G	S	G	J	L
N	Q	L	P	Y	E	K	C	O	H	K	A	Q	Y
Y	M	M	U	R	E	K	O	O	N	S	M	F	P

ARCHERY	CHESS	GOLF	POKER	SKATING
BACCARAT	CRIBBAGE	HOCKEY	POLO	SNAP
BINGO	CROQUET	JUDO	PONTOON	SNOOKER
BOWLS	CURLING	LACROSSE	POOL	SOLO
BRAG	DARTS	MAHJONG	ROULETTE	SQUASH
BRIDGE	DICE	MARBLES	RUMMY	WHIST
CANASTA	FENCING	PELOTA	SHINTY	

BOYS' NAMES

The four 6-letter words have been jumbled. Solve the four anagrams of boys' names and then transfer the shaded letters to the top line of the key anagram, re-arranging them to find a fifth boys' name.

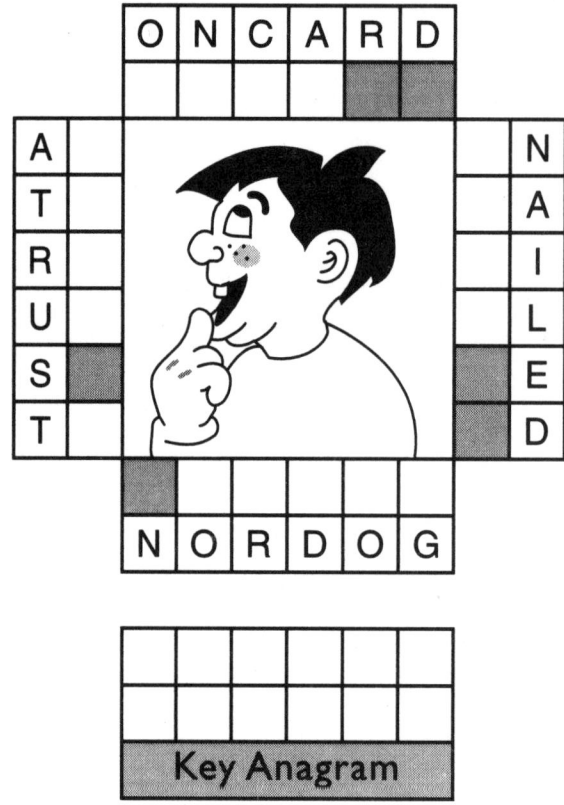

| O | N | C | A | R | D |

| A |
| T |
| R |
| U |
| S |
| T |

| N |
| A |
| I |
| L |
| E |
| D |

| N | O | R | D | O | G |

Key Anagram

TWENTY PHRASES

Each three-word phrase has been hidden by removing the initial letters of each word and then removing the space between them.

For example: ODDS AND ENDS
would become DDSNDNDS

and THREE POINT TURN
would become HREEOINTURN

Solve the three-word phrases listed below.

1. EADVEREELS

2. NHENOW

3. ADEOEASURE

4. INEAYSONDER

5. UTFAVOUR

6. EVENEADLYINS

7. OOLDSARRED

8. ETOUSIC

9. IRDFREY

10. OEEED

11. NHEHELF

12. OUNDHEWIST

13. UTFLACE

14. AKESEAD

15. POATE

16. NDERHEEATHER

17. ETTASE

18. NHEEVEL

19. ACKNDORTH

20. OATCHN

SOLVE THE CLUES

The answers to all thirty clues are words which can be made using these letters:

M T R O L A E F

Example: Part of the foot (3); Answer: TOE

1. Blaze (5)
2. Upright (5)
3. Following (5)
4. On your toes (5)
5. Ceremonial (6)
6. Border (5)
7. Behind time (4)
8. Part of a tree (4)
9. Masculine (4)
10. Spoil (3)
11. Eating occasion (4)
12. Chemical element (5)
13. Confidence or spirit (6)
14. Attic (4)
15. Earthling (5)
16. Royal domain (5)
17. Actor's part (4)
18. Sticky material (3)
19. Drink or meal (3)
20. Noble (4)
21. Type of tree (3)
22. Hesitate (6)
23. Intense flame (5)
24. Young horse (4)
25. Female horse (4)
26. Ditch surrounding a castle (4)
27. Type of hotel (5)
28. Measurement of paper (4)
29. Liquefy (4)
30. Stronghold (4)

CROSSWORD TWO

CLUES

Across

1. Joint connecting hand with forearm (5)
6. Game similar to hockey, played on horseback (4)
7. A type of fruit (4)
8. Unit of length equalling 1760 yards (4)
10. Liberate (4)
12. Curved structure as support for bridge (4)
14. Military land force of a nation (4)
15. Leave out (4)
16. Stalk (4)
17. Strong alloy based on iron (5)

Down

2. A person who commands (5)
3. Warmest season of the year (6)
4. Tall structure (5)
5. Vehicle for several passengers (5)
9. Arrangement of material for the page of a newspaper, for example (6)
10. Frozen dew (5)
11. Keen (5)
13. Sound of a bell (5)

GIRLS' NAMES

The four 6-letter words have been jumbled. Solve the four anagrams of girls' names and then transfer the shaded letters to top line of the key anagram, re-arranging them to find a fifth girls' name.

```
        G O M I N E
        H           I
        I           N
        D           S
        J           E
        U           E
        T           D
        H E C A R L
```


Key Anagram

COMPOSERS

Find the names of composers listed below in the grid, reading forwards, backwards, horizontally, vertically or diagonally, but always in a straight line.

M	B	R	A	H	M	S	T	I	D	L	A	V	I	V
T	E	B	I	Z	E	T	S	N	I	P	O	H	C	T
R	E	N	G	A	W	R	L	I	S	Z	T	F	F	X
R	T	I	D	X	D	A	O	C	S	O	W	M	R	P
B	H	T	R	E	B	U	H	C	S	B	B	O	R	A
N	O	G	A	P	L	S	S	U	A	O	K	O	Q	D
B	V	E	R	A	E	S	C	P	X	R	K	E	G	T
A	E	I	N	G	A	C	S	A	M	O	Z	A	R	T
C	N	R	E	A	M	V	I	O	F	D	A	F	R	Y
H	T	G	L	N	X	W	B	I	H	I	T	A	I	M
D	V	L	G	I	T	T	E	Z	I	N	O	D	A	X
D	D	E	A	N	O	V	L	H	F	Y	D	H	D	M
G	Z	H	R	I	H	Z	I	O	J	W	L	Y	F	E
B	I	A	X	D	C	S	U	I	L	E	D	N	A	H
O	D	R	A	T	I	Z	S	R	R	A	V	E	L	H

ARNE

BACH

BEETHOVEN

BERLIOZ

BIZET

BORODIN

BRAHMS

CHOPIN

DELIUS

DONIZETTI

ELGAR

GRIEG

HANDEL

HAYDN

HOLST

LEHAR

LISZT

MAHLER

MASCAGNI

MENDELSSOHN

MOZART

PAGANINI

PROKOFIEV

PUCCINI

RAVEL

SCHUBERT

SIBELIUS

STRAUSS

VERDI

VIVALDI

WAGNER

COMPLETE-A-CROSSWORD

Complete the crossword by inserting the 26 letters of the alphabet once each only.

BOYS AND GIRLS

Find the starting point and move from square to square horizontally and vertically, but not diagonally, to spell out a girl's name followed by a boy's name. You are looking for five boys and five girls. Use every square once, and finish at the top, right-hand square. Your journey will take you in a clockwise direction.

NE	S	AN	GE	LA	ON
VA	SA	HN	RE	SI	M
ER	J	O	B	E	CC
ET	P	EP	ST	T	A
B	EL	HE	NA	HO	M
NA	AN	N	IA	D	AS

CROSSWORD THREE

CLUES

Across

3. A large painting on a wall (5)
6. Standard or rational (6)
7. Small legendary creature (5)
8. Tropical lizard (6)
12. Join on to (6)
13. Greek holiday island (5)
14. Look up to (6)
15. Small routine task (5)

Down

1. Common gastropod (5)
2. Quarrel (5)
3. Relative size or extent (9)
4. Arm bone (4)
5. Pinnacle of achievement (4)
9. Small log hut (5)
10. Wool-bearing animal (5)
11. Nocturnal insect (4)
12. At a great distance (4)

ANIMALS

The four 6-letter words have been jumbled. Solve the four anagrams of animals and then transfer the shaded letters to top line of the key anagram, re-arranging them to find a fifth animal.

C	O	Y	T	O	E

A M I L A P

O N A B O B

D	E	N	Y	K	O

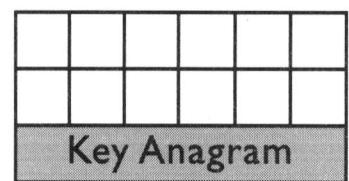

Key Anagram

CRISS-CROSS

With the aid of the clues, complete the criss-cross in each puzzle by inserting the letters provided.

Clue: Town in Australia

Clue: Tied in the kitchen!

Clue: Cold spot

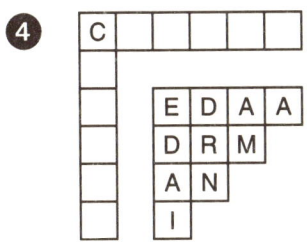

Clue: Say cheese!

Clue: Scary tale

Clue: Sporting contest

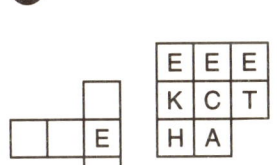

Clue: Behave yourself!

Clue: City in the USA

Clue: Pack your suitcase!

Clue: That's a relief!

Clue: Stretch of water

Clue: Wet jets!

Treasure Hunt

To reach the treasure chest you must first find the starting square and then, by following the compass directions – which will take you once through each of the remaining squares– you will eventually arrive at the treasure. '1E' means one square East, '4S' means four squares South.

1S 2E	2S 4E	1W 1S	3S 2W	2S 4W	3W 2S
4E 1N	1E 3S	2W 2S	1E 2S	1N 2W	1N 2W
2E 3S	2N 4E		2E 3S	1E 2S	1S 2W
1E 3N	1N 2E	2N 2W	2W 1S	2N 1E	1S 2W
1S 3E	1S 3E	2N 2E	2W 1S	4W 1S	3N 2W
3N 1E	1N 3E	1N 2W	2N 2E	2N 2W	5N 5W

BUBBLE AND SQUEAK

Which of the following is not an anagram of
BUBBLE AND SQUEAK?

BEAN BULBS QUAKED

BULB BAN SQUEAKED

DEBUNK A SQUABBLE

QUEEN BAKED BULBS

BAD BULB ASK QUEEN

SQUABBLE BAN DUKE

NUKE BAD SQUABBLE

HOMONYMS

A homonym is a word which has the same sound
as another, but has a different meaning and
spelling. For example, the words RIGHT, RITE,
WRITE and WRIGHT are all homonyms.
Find the pairs of homonyms from these clues:

1. Couple, fruit

2. Visitor, surmised

3. Rod, procession

4. Street, propelled with oar

5. Plunder, musical instrument

6. Construct, invoiced

7. Gaze, step

8. Actual, totter

9. Cavalier, darkness

10. Cruise, auction

RHYMING PAIRS

The answer to each clue is a rhyming pair of
words. Example: Unhappy young man = Sad lad

1. Chubby idiot

2. Small snack

3. Perfectly correct

4. Not at any time

5. Silent revolution

6. Spacious building for cars

7. Twice as much disturbance

8. Moderately cold body of water

9. Distant celestial body

10. 23.00 hours plane journey

11. Counterfeit coins

12. Minor alarm

13. Sensible Scandinavian

14. Fast deception

MAGIC WORD SQUARE

The answer to each clue is a five-letter word. All words can be read both horizontally and vertically.

1	2	3	4	5
2				
3				
4				
5				

1. Of the nose

2. The capital of Ghana

3. Utensil used for serving ice cream

4. Got up

5. Folded-back jacket collar

COUNTRIES

Find the countries listed below in the grid, reading forwards, backwards, horizontally, vertically or diagonally, but always in a straight line.

AFGHANISTAN

ALBANIA

ARGENTINA

AUSTRALIA

AUSTRIA

BANGLADESH

BRAZIL

BULGARIA

CANADA

CHILE

CUBA

DENMARK

FINLAND

FRANCE

GREECE

INDONESIA

MALI

NIGERIA

PAKISTAN

POLAND

PORTUGAL

SPAIN

SWITZERLAND

THAILAND

VENEZUELA

A	L	E	U	Z	E	N	E	V	Q	E	V	B
F	E	K	A	U	S	T	R	A	L	I	A	R
G	C	B	U	L	G	A	R	I	A	N	L	A
H	E	D	M	D	B	G	H	Z	G	I	B	Z
A	E	N	R	U	E	C	I	L	A	M	A	I
N	R	A	C	N	A	D	A	N	A	C	N	L
I	G	L	T	I	N	D	O	N	E	S	I	A
S	W	I	T	Z	E	R	L	A	N	D	A	G
T	N	A	T	S	I	K	A	P	H	U	P	U
A	C	H	H	A	U	S	T	R	I	A	S	T
N	C	T	D	E	N	M	A	R	K	G	F	R
D	N	A	L	N	I	F	R	A	N	C	E	O
N	I	G	E	R	I	A	D	N	A	L	O	P

CROSSWORD FOUR

CLUES

Across
1. Not heavy (5)
5. Secure (4)
6. Woman's hat tied by ribbons (6)
7. An exclamation of grief or alarm (4)
9. A reflective sound (4)
11. Mixture of oats, nuts and fruit eaten with milk (6)
12. Short written message (4)
13. Entice (5)

Down
2. Metal, symbol Fe (4)
3. Good-looking (8)
4. Banquet (5)
5. A headlong rush of cattle (8)
8. Children's comic (5)
10. Applaud (4)

WORD SEARCH

Find 15 parts of the body. Words must be in a straight line in any direction, and letters may be used more than once.

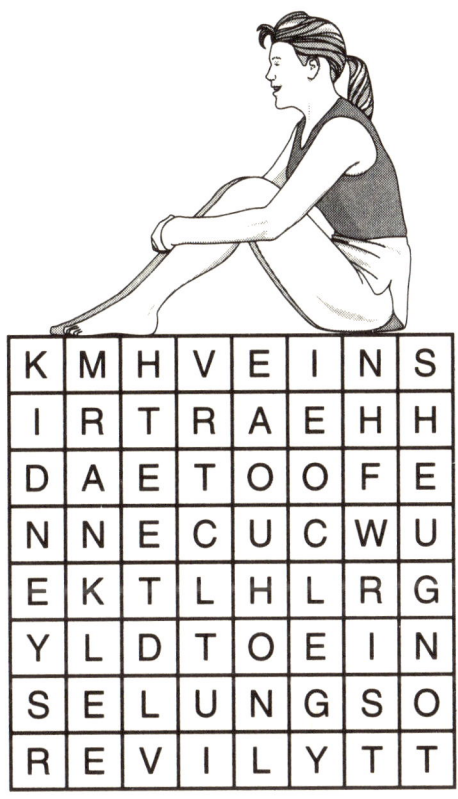

K	M	H	V	E	I	N	S
I	R	T	R	A	E	H	H
D	A	E	T	O	O	F	E
N	N	E	C	U	C	W	U
E	K	T	L	H	L	R	G
Y	L	D	T	O	E	I	N
S	E	L	U	N	G	S	O
R	E	V	I	L	Y	T	T

TREES

Find eight trees in this narrative:

A BEE CHASED ME AND MY PAL, WILL OWEN.
FIRST I FELL IN THE RIVER. I WAS SOAKED.
THEN, AS HE ATE A PIPPIN EACH DAY, HE SAID,
'MA, PLEASE FIND MY HELMET.'

TRANSMUTATION

Turn HEAT into FIRE in five moves.

H E A T

_ _ _ _

_ _ _ _

_ _ _ _

F I R E

WORD

Find a five-letter word which, when placed in front
of each of these six words, makes new words:

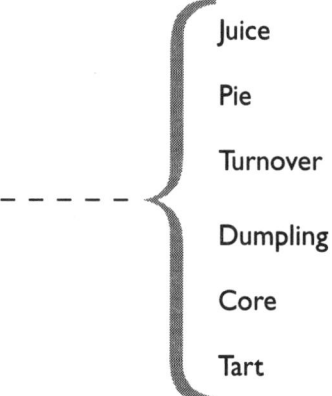

Juice

Pie

Turnover

Dumpling

Core

Tart

MATCHES

Construct four squares using 24 matches.

NUMBERS

If you were to write down all the numbers from
0 to 60, how many times would you write the
number 5?

SETS

Re-arrange these objects into 4 groups of four.

MANGO

JASMINE

RUBY

QUINCE

PANSY

EAGLE

FALCON

DIAMOND

KINGFISHER

AZALEA

LILY

SAPPHIRE

GULL

PINEAPPLE

KIWI

AGATE

HEXAGRAM

Re-arrange the letters to form the names of six colours.
Transfer the shaded letters to the key anagram and then re-arrange them to form a seventh colour.

N O G A R E

N O G D I I

L E V T O I

L O W L E Y

D E G L O N

V I S R E L

Key Anagram

ZZZZ

Find eight or more words by following the lines to the circled letters. Each word must include a Z. Letters may be used more than once in a word.

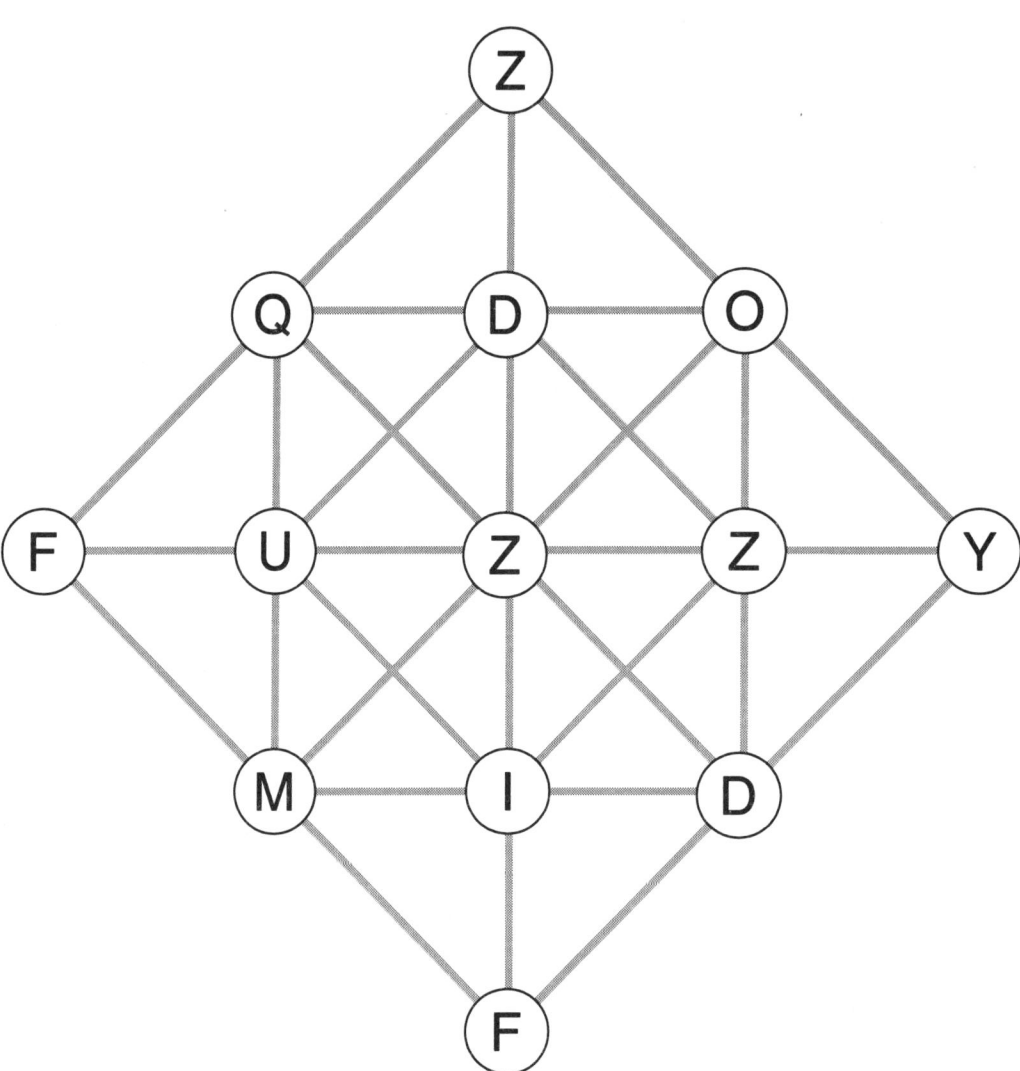

SQUARE

Place the six pieces into the square without overlapping.

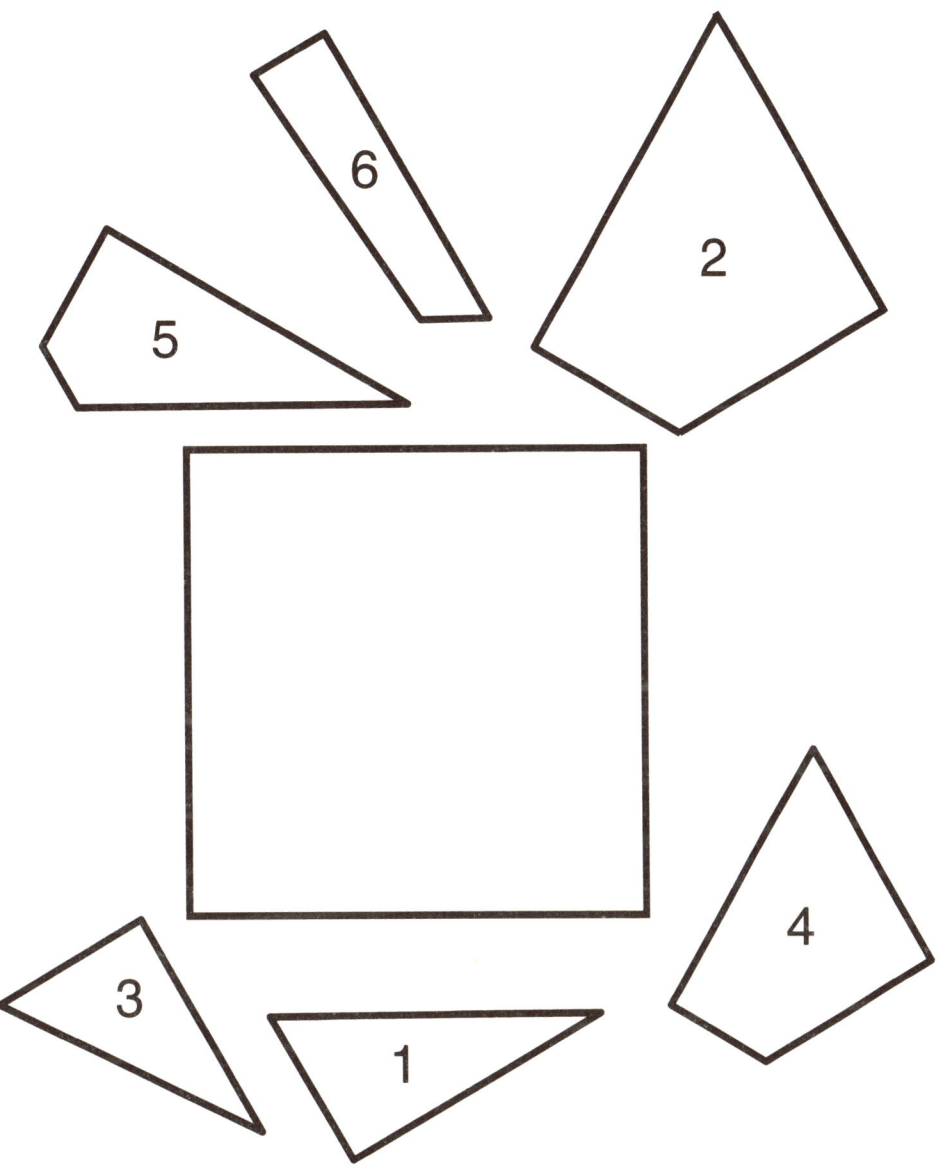

OCTAGON

Pair up sets of three-letter words to make 8 six-letter words.

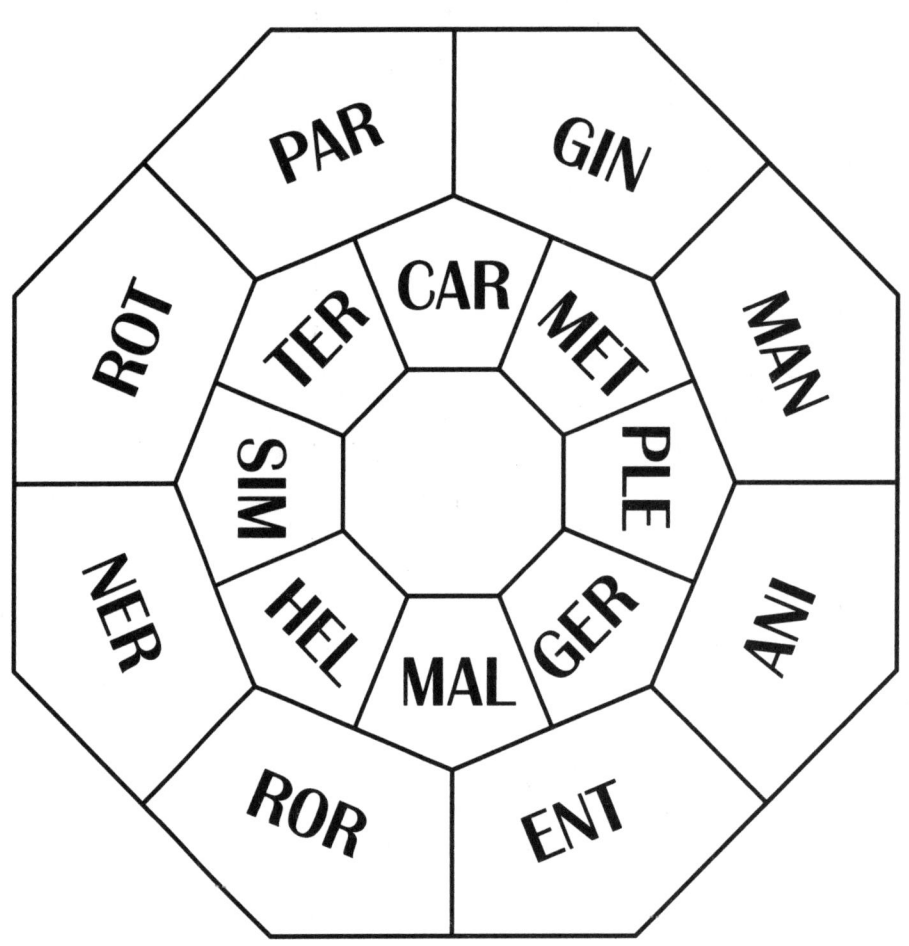

PENTAGRAM

Re-arrange the letters to form 5 boys' names. Transfer the shaded letters into the key anagram, then re-arrange them to form a sixth boy's name.

Key Anagram

HONEYCOMB

Find 15 animals by tracing out adjacent letters.
You can double a letter or use the same letter more than once in each word.

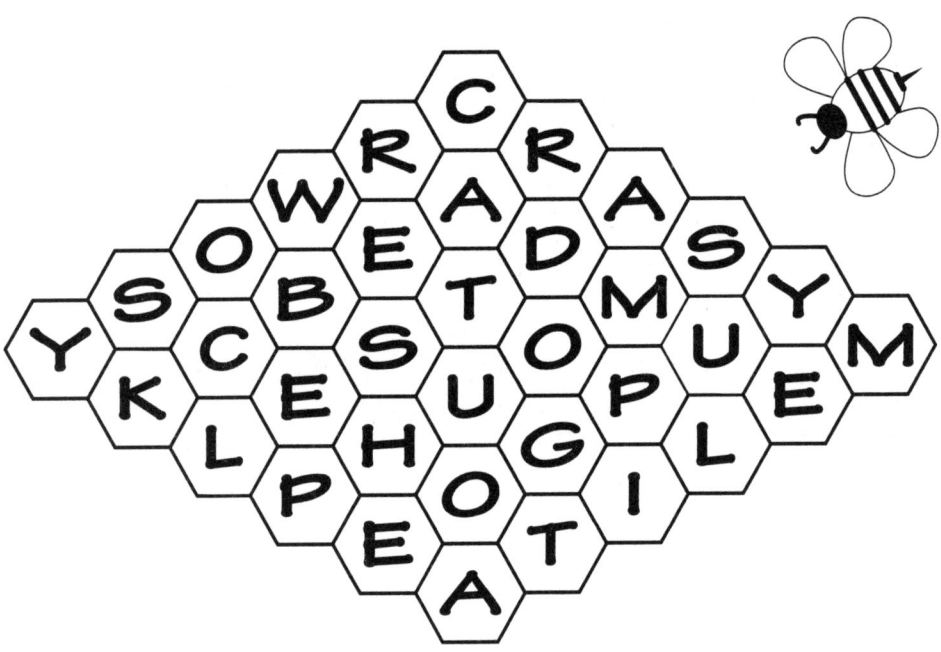

WORD SEARCH

Find 20 living creatures in the grid. Words can be found in any direction, but always in a straight line.

Z	W	O	L	L	A	W	S
E	X	C	I	O	R	C	E
B	S	A	O	E	O	E	F
R	A	M	N	R	B	R	F
A	P	R	P	T	O	L	A
D	D	I	C	G	A	W	R
B	O	A	G	Y	X	O	I
N	G	E	E	M	U	N	G

107

HONEYCOMB

Go from hexagon to adjacent hexagon to find 12 birds in the honeycomb.
You can double a letter or use the same letter more than once in each word.

BOXES

Which of the five boxes labelled A, B, C, D and E has most in common with the first box?

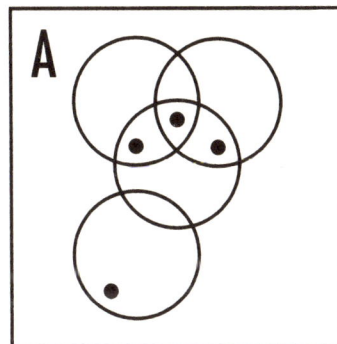

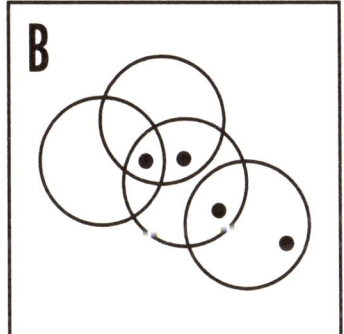

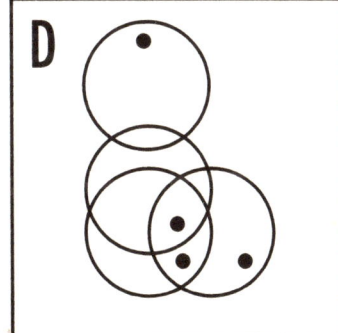

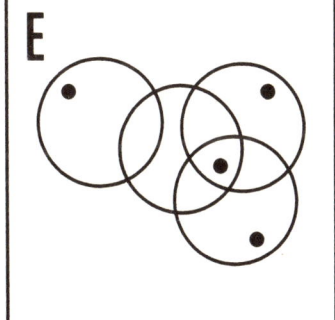

FRUITS CROSSWORD

Place the names of the fruits in the crossword.
Hint: Place the 5-letter words first.

CROSSWORD FIVE

CLUES

Across

1. Rotate rapidly on an axis (4)
3. Make less distinct (4)
6. Jog (4)
8. Composition in verse (4)
9. Gain knowledge (5)
10. Person who plays a part (5)
12. Skin irritation (4)
13. Discover (4)
14. Level (4)
15. Type of fruit (4)

Down

1. Man-made device orbiting the earth (9)
2. Object of worship (4)
4. King of the beasts (4)
5. Part left over (9)
7. Educate (5)
8. Conclusive evidence (5)
10. Dull pain (4)
11. Food in plentiful supply in Asia (4)

Crossword One *page 80*

Colours *page 82*

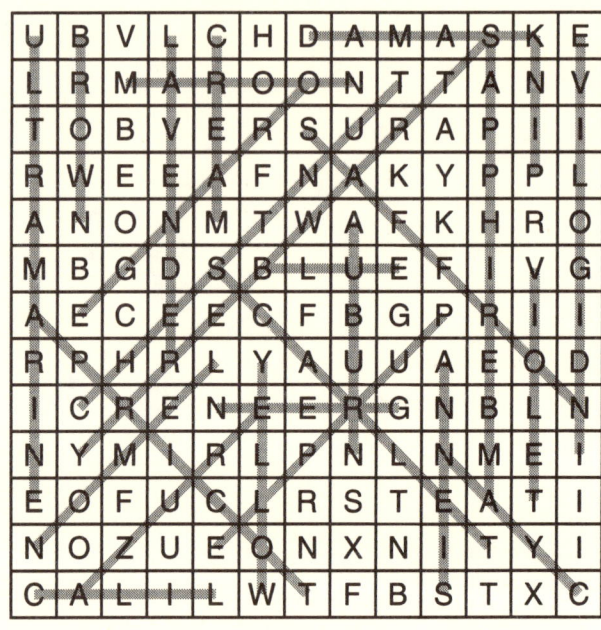

Name Game *page 81*

George	Gilbert
Martin	Christopher
Sebastian	Kathleen
Ingrid	Thelma
Pamela	Malcolm
Nicholas	Christian
Marian	Rosalind
Alistair	Eleanor
Granville	Douglas
Selina	Nathaniel
Graham	Rachel
Natalie	Sandra
Reginald	Donald
Gillian	Sharon
Christine	Geoffrey
Clifford	Maxine
Priscilla	Annabelle

Games *page 83*

SKATING does not appear in the grid.

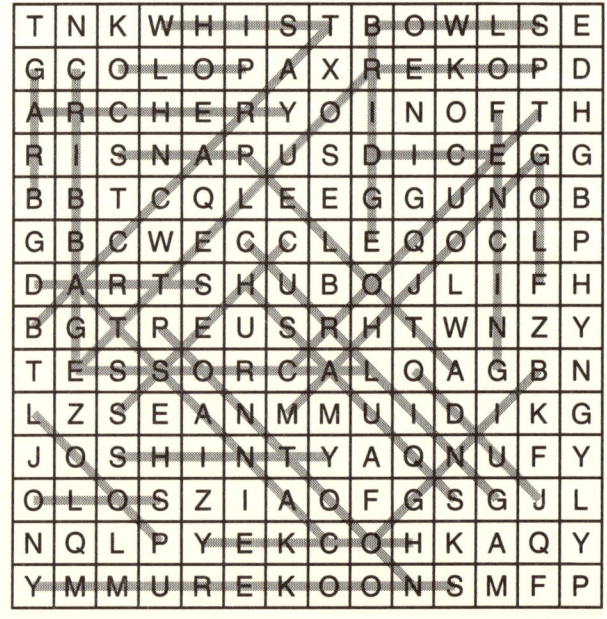

Route 66 *page 00*

Illinois	Missouri
Kansas	Oklahoma
Texas	New Mexico
Arizona	California

Boys' Names *page 84*

Conrad
Stuart
Gordon
Daniel
Key Anagram: Gerald

Crossword Two *page 86*

Twenty Phrases *page 85*

1. Head over heels
2. In the know
3. Made to measure
4. Nine-days wonder
5. Out of favour
6. Seven deadly sins
7. No holds barred
8. Set to music
9. Bird of prey
10. To see red
11. On the shelf
12. Round the twist
13. Out of place
14. Take as read
15. Up-to-date
16. Under the weather
17. Set at ease
18. On the level
19. Back and forth
20. To catch on

Girls' Names *page 87*

Imogen
Judith
Denise
Rachel
Key Anagram: Muriel

Composers *page 88*

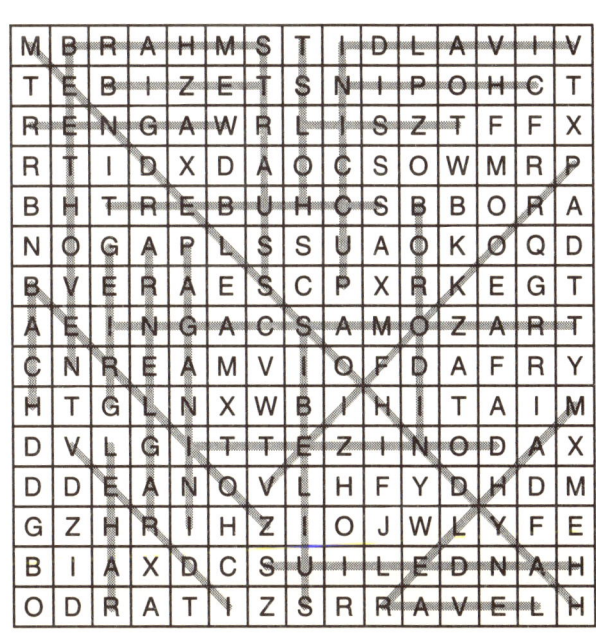

Solve the Clues *page 85*

1. Flame
2. Moral
3. After
4. Alert
5. Formal
6. Frame
7. Late
8. Leaf
9. Male
10. Mar
11. Meal
12. Metal
13. Morale
14. Loft
15. Mortal
16. Realm
17. Role
18. Tar
19. Tea
20. Earl
21. Elm
22. Falter
23. Flare
24. Foal
25. Mare
26. Moat
27. Motel
28. Ream
29. Melt
30. Fort

Complete-a-Crossword *page 89*

Boys and Girls *page 90*

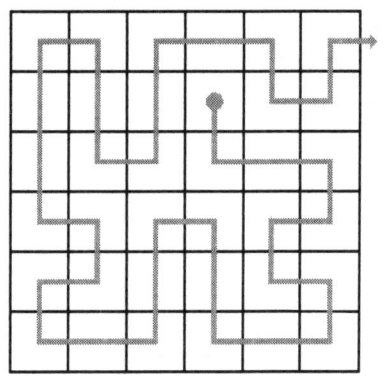

Rebecca, Thomas, Diana, Stephen, Annabel, Peter,
Vanessa, John, Angela, Simon

Crossword Three *page 91*

Animals *page 92*

Coyote
Impala
Baboon
Donkey
Key anagram: Monkey

Criss-Cross *page 93*

1. Alice Springs
2. Apron strings
3. Arctic Circle
4. Candid Camera
5. Ghost story
6. Olympic Games
7. Keep the peace
8. Salt Lake City
9. Holiday camp
10. Thank Heavens!
11. Pacific Ocean
12. Water pistols

Treasure Hunt *page 94*

Visit the squares in the following sequence:

14	17	2	10	24	35
23	3	15	7	1	9
25	34	🧰	12	5	18
16	11	22	19	8	29
27	20	4	30	32	6
33	31	26	28	21	13

Bubble and Squeak *page 95*

QUEEN BAKED BULBS

Homonyms *page 95*

1. pair / pear
2. guest / guessed
3. cue / queue
4. road / rowed
5. loot / lute
6. build / billed
7. stare / stair
8. real / reel
9. knight / night
10. sail / sale

Rhyming Pairs *page 95*

1. Plump chump
2. Light bite
3. Quite right
4. Never ever
5. Quiet riot
6. Large garage
7. Double trouble
8. Cool pool
9. Far star
10. Night flight
11. Funny money
12. Slight fright
13. Sane Dane
14. Quick trick

Magic Word Square *page 96*

N	A	S	A	L
A	C	C	R	A
S	C	O	O	P
A	R	O	S	E
L	A	P	E	L

Countries *page 97*

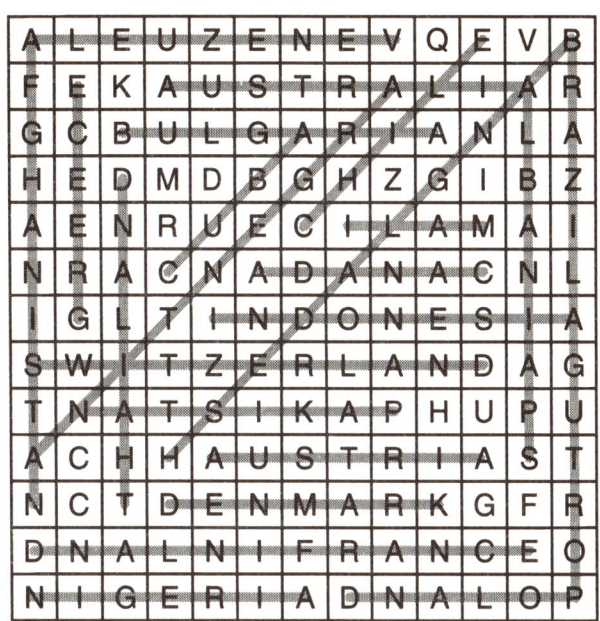

Crossword Four *page 98*

Word Search *page 99*

Tongue	Kidneys	Lungs
Shoulder	Veins	Leg
Chest	Wrist	Arm
Heart	Ankle	Toe
Liver	Foot	Teeth

Trees *page 100*

Tree names are shown in bold type:

A **BEE CH**ASED ME AND MY PAL,
WILL OWEN. **FIR**ST I FELL IN THE RIVER.
I WAS S**OAK**ED. THEN, **AS HE** ATE A
PIP**PIN E**ACH DAY, HE SAID, "**MA PLE**ASE
FIND MY H**ELM**ET."

Transmutation *page 100*

H E A T
H E A D
H E R D
H E R E
H I R E
F I R E

Word *page 100*

Apple

Matches *page 100*

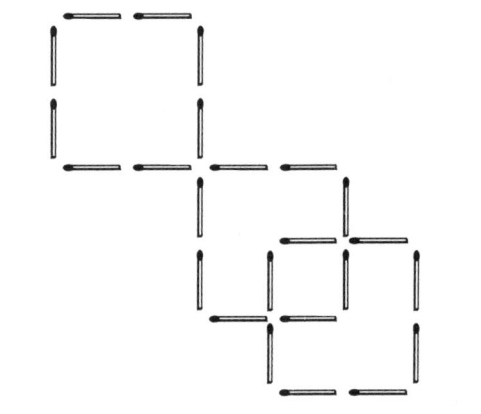

Numbers *page 100*

16

Sets *page 100*

Fruit	*Jewels*	*Flowers*	*Birds*
Mango	Ruby	Pansy	Falcon
Kiwi	Diamond	Lily	Gull
Quince	Sapphire	Jasmine	Kingfisher
Pineapple	Agate	Azalea	Eagle

Hexagram *page 101*

Orange
Violet
Golden
Silver
Yellow
Indigo
Key anagram: Sienna

ZZZZ *page 102*

Quiz	Fizzy	Fuzz
Muzzy	Fuzzy	Dozy
Fizz	Dizzy	Zoo

Square *page 103*

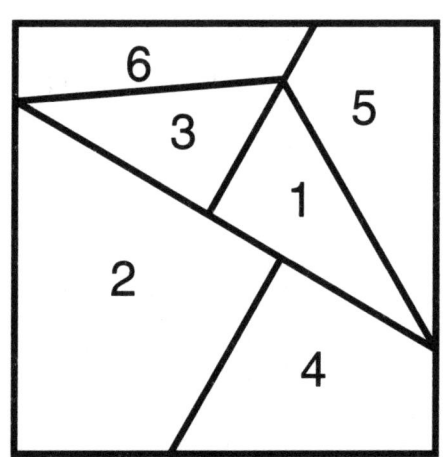

Octagon page 104

PARENT	GINGER
MANNER	HELMET
CARROT	TERROR
ANIMAL	SIMPLE

Pentagram page 105

Robert Arnold

Andrew Graham

Dennis

Key Anagram: Gerald

Honeycomb page 106

Cat	Bear	Sow
Dog	Pig	Elk
Rat	Cow	Ram
Mouse	Sheep	Ass
Ewe	Goat	Mule

Word Search page 107

Giraffe	Frog	Zebra
Scorpion	Swallow	Gnu
Bee	Wren	Crab
Goat	Boa	Owl
Doe	Dog	Emu
Ox	Pig	Ram
Lion	Ant	

Honeycomb page 108

Thrush	Rook	Magpie
Kiwi	Wren	Duck
Goose	Hen	Pigeon
Hawk	Crow	Geese

Boxes page 109

C.

There is black spot where 3 circles intersect

There is black spot where 2 circles intersect

There is black spot in 1 circle where 3 circles intersect

There is black spot in 1 circle where 2 circles intersect

Fruits Crossword page 110

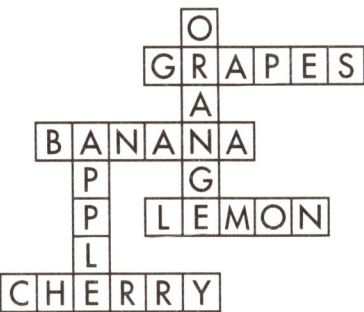

Crossword Five page 111

JUST FOR FUN

NO SQUARES

If you consider only the 22 solid lines in this diagram, no squares of any size appear in the grid. How many of the 18 dotted lines can you turn into solid lines without making a square of any size appear?

MIND-READING TRICK

Pick a number from 1–10

Multiply by 9

Subtract 5

Add the digits, then add again until you are left with a one-digit number

Pick the letter of the alphabet which corresponds with that letter (A = 1, B = 2, etc)

Think of a country beginning with that letter

Think of an animal whose name begins with the second letter of that country

Think of a colour associated with that animal
Now turn to the answer section on page 128

THE EXASPERATING 'GRY' PUZZLE

Think of common words ending in GRY – HUNGRY and ANGRY are two of them. There are three words in the English language, what is the third word?

BOLD PRUSSIAN

What is unusual about this sentence:

SHOW THIS BOLD PRUSSIAN THAT PRAISES SLAUGHTER – SLAUGHTER BRINGS ROUT.

ISSUES

What is unusual about this sentence?

ISSUES TOPPING OUR MAIL; MANSLAUGHTER

HANGMAN

Each player in turn becomes the 'hangman', and chooses a word, then writes in the blanks. So 'MEMBERSHIP' becomes (– – – – – – – – –)

The second player then selects a letter – for example, S – and the 'hangman' writes in all occurrences of the letter. In the example, there is just one: (– – – – – S – – –).

The second player then selects another letter – A, say – and because there is no A, the 'hangman' builds the first part of the scaffold.

The game progresses until either the second player has found the word or been 'hanged'.

The sequence of building the scaffold is:

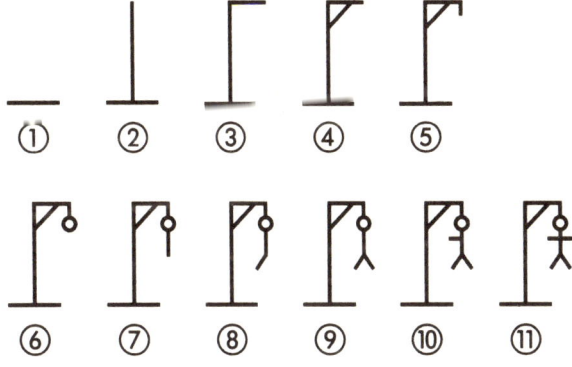

The 'hangman' wins after the eleventh wrong guess. The game can be extended to include 'famous people', 'song titles', 'places', etc.

TWO DOORS

During a recent visit to a London department store, I saw the following notices on two adjacent doors. What did they mean?

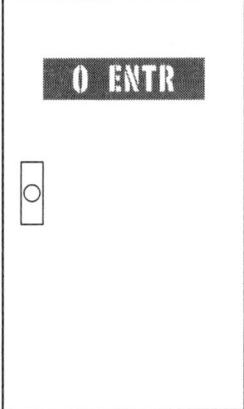

CONFESSIONS

1. The players sit round in a circle and each is given a long strip of paper and pen or pencil.

2. Everyone then writes his or her name on the top line, which is then folded over so the top name is not revealed.

3. Next, everyone passes the paper around the circle of players in the same direction and after a while someone shouts 'Stop!' Each player then writes down 'a confession' on the paper.

4. The papers are again passed round the circle, after once more being folded, and eventually someone shouts 'Stop!' again.

5. This time the players write on the paper the 'reason why' they did it.

6. The papers are then passed on for a final time, after which they are unfolded and the person holding the paper reads out the three sections.

Naturally, there are often some hilarious results!

VISUAL TRICKERY

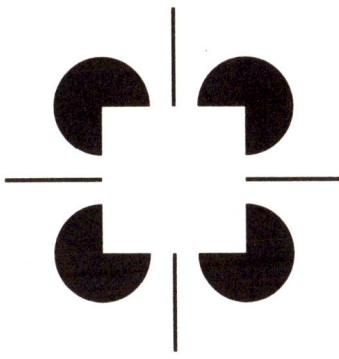

The square exists in the eye of the beholder, but not on the paper.

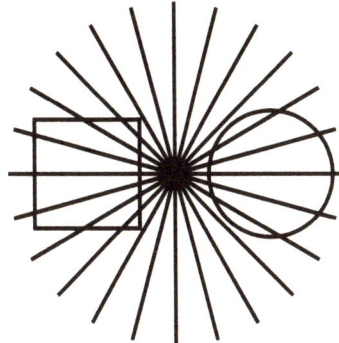

The figure on the left is a perfect square and the figure opposite a perfect circle.

This figure includes an embedded hexagon. But where?

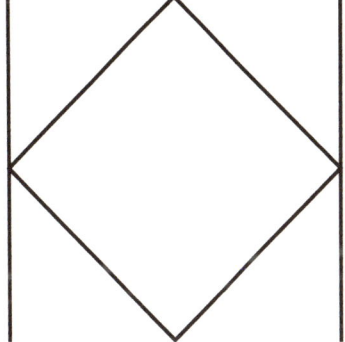

This is, of course, a diamond between uprights. But could it equally be the letter K with mirror image or the letter W on top of the letter M?

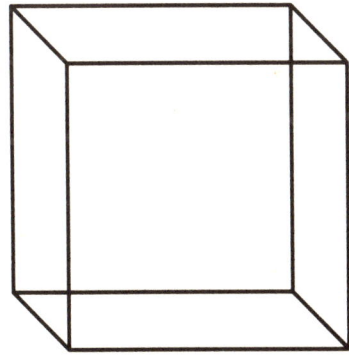

The 'Necker' cube – if you stare hard at it for a short while, the image will reverse

The four vertical lines are parallel.

The answer to each set of five clues is the name of a country. The sooner you can answer, the more points you score.

1. It is bisected by the equator (5 points)
   The official languages are Swahili and English (4 points)
   Uganda is to the west and Tanzania to the south (3 points)
   It has an oil refinery at Mombasa (2 points)
   The capital is Nairobi (1 point)

2. Its flag consists of 3 horizontal bands; white, green, red (5 points)
   It is a republic of Eastern Europe (4 points)
   Its capital is Sofia (3 points)
   It is bounded to the east by the Black Sea (2 points)
   An anagram of its name is BIG LAURA (1 point)

3. Its parliament is called Folketing (5 points)
   It is a kingdom of Northern Europe (4 points)
   Its flag is red with a white cross (3 points)
   The unit of currency is the krone (2 points)
   The capital is Copenhagen (1 point)

4. It is on the African continent (5 points)
   Much of the country is desert (4 points)
   Arabic is the official language (3 points)
   Rabat is the capital (2 points)
   Its largest city is Casablanca (1 point)

5. It was discovered in 1497 by Sebastian Cabot (5 points)
   Parliament consists of a Senate and a House of Commons (4 points)
   It is a large producer of gold, silver and uranium (3 points)
   It has a large inlet called Hudson Bay (2 points)
   It has provinces called Manitoba, Nova Scotia and Saskatchewan (1 point)

6. Its national anthem is 'May Glory Crown Our Illustrious Sovereign' (5 points)
   It lies between India and Tibet on the slopes of the Himalayas (4 points)
   It is the birthplace of Buddah (3 points)
   Its highest peak is Mount Everest (2 points)
   An anagram of its name is PLANE (1 point)

7. It gained independence from Spain in 1830 (5 points)
   The unit of currency is the Bolivar (4 points)
   It is a South American republic (3 points)
   The Orinoco is its principal river (2 points)
   The capital is Caracas (1 point)

8. From 1946 to 1991 it was a one-party communist state (5 points)
   Its flag is a black two-headed eagle on a red background (4 points)
   It is situated on the Adriatic Sea to the north of Greece (3 points)
   Its currency is the Lek (2 points)
   The capital is Tirana (1 point)

9. The national anthem, translated, means 'To Battle, Men of Bayamo' (5 points)
   Its main export is sugar (4 points)
   The government of General Batista was overthrown in 1959 (3 points)
   It is the largest island in the Caribbean (2 points)
   The capital is Havana (1 point)

10. It has an area of 1.58 sq km (5 points)
    Its capital is Vaduz (4 points)
    It is a principality on the Upper Rhine (3 points)
    It lies between Austria and Switzerland (2 points)
    An anagram of its name is THE NICEST LINE (1 point)

NAMYSTICS

Namystics first appeared in the 1920s. They can be played with your own name, place names, famous people, etc. All you need is a blank outline like this:

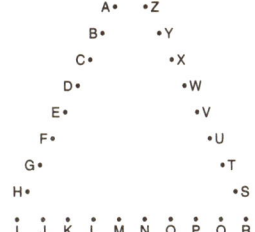

Starting with the first letter of the chosen name draw a straight line to the second letter, then to the third, and so on. Double letters are treated as if they were a single letter. When you have finished fill in any enclosed areas and see what unique pattern is created. The two examples below show the names of the authors of this book.

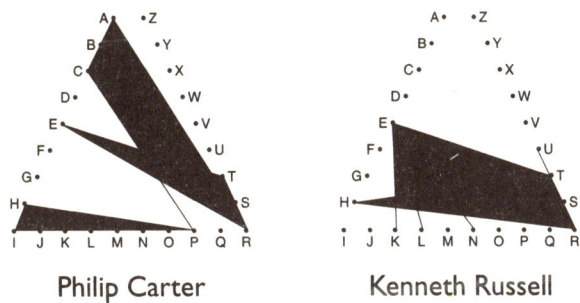

Philip Carter   Kenneth Russell

Now, see if you can identify the following six namystics, which are all Shakespeare characters:

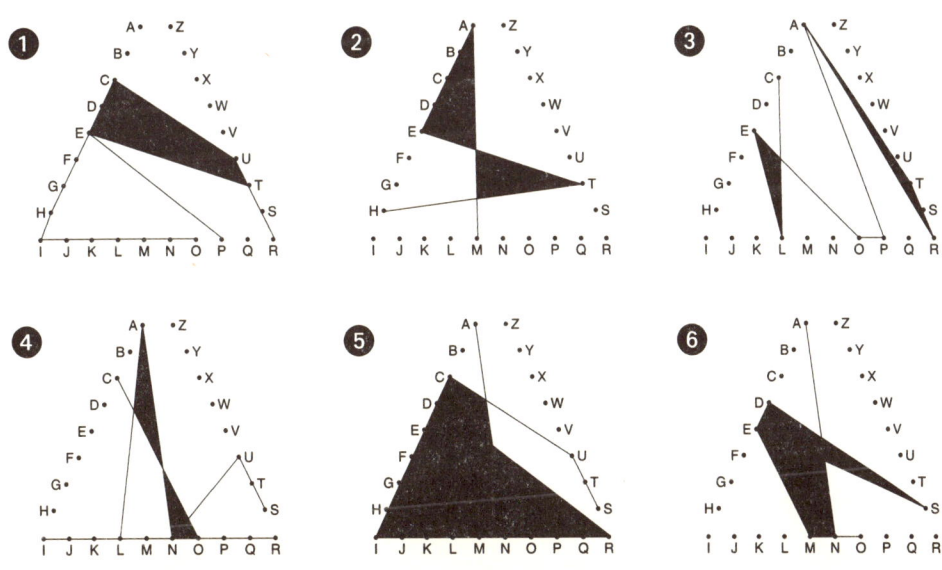

JOKES

Snow White received a camera for her birthday and happily took pictures of all the Dwarfs. When she finished the first roll of film she took it to the chemist shop to be developed. A week later she went to collect the photographs but was told they were not ready. Snow White was so upset that she began to cry. The shop assistant tried to comfort her and said, 'Don't worry, one day your prints will come.'

Two brothers were being taken to the electric chair to be executed for jointly committing a heinous crime. The elder brother was asked if he had any last requests. 'Just one,' he replied. 'I would like to listen to Lee Marvin singing "Wandering Star" as you're strapping me in the chair and throwing the switch.'
Then the younger brother was asked if he, too, had a last request. 'Just one also,' he replied. 'Would you please execute me first.'

An English journalist was touring the USA. As he was checking out of one hotel he said to the manager, 'What's with that Indian chief sitting in the lobby? He's been here since I arrived.'
'That's the famous "Big Chief Forget-Me-Not",' replied the manager. 'The hotel is built on an Indian reservation and part of the agreement is to allow the chief free use of the premises for the rest of his life. He is 92 and can remember every slightest detail of his life.'
The journalist decided to put this to the test and said to the chief, 'What did you have for breakfast on your 21st birthday?'
'Eggs,' said the chief without hesitation, and the journalist was duly impressed.
Some years later, on his return to the same hotel,

the journalist was somewhat surprised to see "Big Chief Forget-Me-Not" still sitting there and decided to greet him in the traditional manner. 'How!' said the journalist.
'Scrambled,' said the chief.

Q. Why should you never swim in the river in Paris?
A. Because to do so would be in Seine.

Q. What is the best way for a ghost hunter to keep fit?
A. Exorcise regularly.

Q. What did Lot do when his wife was turned into a block of salt?
A. He put her in the cellar.

Q. What turned the moon pale?
A. Atmos-fear.

Q. What does the sea say to the sand?
A. Not a lot – it mostly waves.

FUNNY STORIES AND CURIOUS FACTS

A man was seriously injured in Wesley Chapel, Florida, when he was hit in the leg with pieces of a bullet which he fired at the exhaust pipe of his car. When repairing the car, he had needed to bore a hole in the pipe. When he couldn't find a drill, he tried to shoot a hole in it.

In Nevada, a bank robber called Eddie Blake slid a note to the cashier. 'This is a hold-up,' it announced. 'Put all the money into a bag and hand it over.'
The woman complied and Blake made his getaway. An hour later he arrived home to find the police waiting for him. His demand note had been written on the back of an envelope which contained his name and address.

During the Napoleonic Wars a ship arrived in the North East of England from France. On board, when unloading the goods, the crew found a monkey stowaway. The monkey was handed over to the constabulary who decided that the monkey was French. After a short trial the monkey was condemned and hung because England was at war with France.

In 1922 a man in Newton, North Carolina accidentally shot himself dead when, awakening to the sound of a ringing telephone beside his bed, he reached for it but grabbed instead a Smith & Wesson .38 special which discharged when he put it to his ear.

A jury at a West Country court was forced to retire to the courtroom kitchen because of space shortage. After a while they began to feel cold and decided to switch on the gas oven. Unfortunately, in the heat of the debate they forgot to light it and there was a large explosion. With typical British stiff upper lip and bulldog spirit they loyally continued with their deliberations but had to open the kitchen door in order to breathe. When they eventually returned to court, the judge ruled that an open door did not constitute complete privacy and ordered a retrial.

During jury selection for a trial in the USA, the judge asked potential Juror No 1 if there was any reason he could not be a fair and impartial juror. 'There certainly is,' he replied. 'Juror No 8 is one of my ex-wives and if I were on the same jury, I guarantee you that we could not possibly agree on anything.'
The judge promptly excused both jurors.

PERVERTED PROVERBS

A hair on the head is worth two on the brush.

The early worm gets eaten first.

A stitch in time saves a blush.

You never know what you can do without till you try.

A friend in need is a terrible nuisance.

Where there's a frill, there's a fray.

To play cards is heavenly, to cheat divine.

A set of dominoes consists of 28 pieces (or bones). There are several variations of the game, one of the most interesting being that of 'fives and threes'. The object of this game is to be the first to 61 points. Two or more people can play.

Play:

1. The dominoes are turned upside-down and shuffled. Each player then takes a domino, the highest number deciding the 'down' or first play.

2. The winner of the down then reshuffles the whole pack and selects seven dominoes without revealing them to the other players who then follow suit.

3. After the first hand has been played the shuffle and down procedure is taken in turn and this continues until 61 points has been reached.

The game is played as any ordinary game of dominoes, anyone not being able to play tapping the table to indicate pass. If no one can play, the remaining dominoes of each player are totalled up, the lowest total winning the hand and being awarded the point.

The object of 'fives and threes' is to try and play those dominoes, the exposed ends of which, added together, will produce a number divisible by 5 or 3, or both, without a remainder (as in the examples shown above).

For example: the first player sets down double-five (crossways) for which he scores two points (2 x 5).

The next player puts down a five-two and because the 10 (2 x 5) plus the 2 totals 12, scores 4 points (4 x 3).

The next player lays down the five-three and as the combined ends 2 + 3 total 5, he scores 1 point (1 x 5).

The highest possible scoring move in the game is 15 i.e. double-five at one end and another 5 at the other, for which a score is achieved of 8 points (5 x 3 plus 3 x 5).

SCORE 4
10 + 2 = 12
12 ÷ 3 = 4

SCORE 1
3 + 2 = 5
5 ÷ 5 = 1

A game for two players.

Each player draws his opponent's and his own sea on 8 x 8 squares.

He then draws

I Battleship	4 adjoining squares
2 Cruisers	3 adjoining squares
3 Destroyers	2 adjoining squares
4 Submarines	I square

When he fires 3 shots per turn at his opponent he records the shots in his opponent's sea thus:

    DI   F6   H3

and records the results, in this case none, ie

When his opponent fires 3 shots at his sea, he records the shots, ie

    D4   E6   HI

As a battleship has been hit on E6, he says 'I hit a battleship', but does not say which hit was successful.

The winner is the player who sinks all 10 craft.

Opponent's Sea
(Record your shots and results)

Your Sea
(Record your opponent's shots and results)

No Squares *page 118*

Nine additional lines. This solution shows the maximum number of complete lines possible before a square appears.

Mind-Reading Trick *page 119*

You are thinking of a grey elephant from Denmark!

The Exasperating 'GRY' Puzzle *page 119*

LANGUAGE!!
Look at the wording of the question. The third word in 'the English language' is language. Just for the record, the only two words to end in 'GRY' are ANGRY and HUNGRY.

Bold Prussian *page 119*

It is also a sentence when the first letter of each word is removed:

HOW HIS OLD RUSSIAN HAT RAISES LAUGHTER – LAUGHTER RINGS OUT.

Issues *page 119*

It is still a sentence with alteration of word boundaries and punctuation:

IS SUE STOPPING OUR MAILMAN'S LAUGHTER?

Two Doors *page 120*

Several letters had dropped off. The signs on the doors should have read:

NO ENTRY and GENTLEMEN

Visual Trickery *page 121*

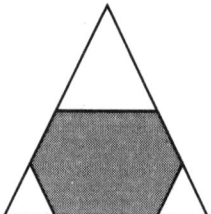

Country Quiz Game *page 122*

1. Kenya	2. Bulgaria
3. Denmark	4. Morocco
5. Canada	6. Nepal
7. Venezuela	8. Albania
9. Cuba	10. Liechtenstein

Namystics *page 123*

1. Petruchio	2. Macbeth
3. Cleopatra	4. Coriolanus
5. Andronicus	6. Desdemona